continued . . .

D1114134

"*Negotiation Generation* is a wonderful book. It offers realistic, practical advice to parents for communicating with and disciplining children in ways that nurture responsibility, accountability, compassion, and respect. Lynne skillfully captures the complexities of parenting with warmth, empathy, clarity, and humor, providing many illustrations that make her points come alive. This book will be read and reread as an invaluable resource for parents of children of all ages. I recommend it highly."

—Robert Brooks, PhD,
Faculty, Harvard Medical School;
Coauthor of *Raising Resilient Children*
and *Raising a Self-Disciplined Child*

"Enormously readable, practical, and helpful . . . a proactive approach. . . . *Negotiation Generation* is full of examples all families can relate to, and it will assist families in creating environments where children thrive. Parents will be able to spend time playing with their growing children . . . not playing catch-up with their growing problems."

—Judith S. Palfrey, MD,
T. Berry Brazelton Professor of Pediatrics,
Harvard Medical School;
Chief, Division of General Pediatrics,
Children's Hospital, Boston

Negotiation
Generation

*Take Back
Your Parental Authority
Without Punishment*

Lynne Reeves Griffin, RN, MEd

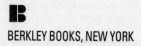

BERKLEY BOOKS, NEW YORK

THE BERKLEY PUBLISHING GROUP
Published by the Penguin Group
Penguin Group (USA) Inc.
375 Hudson Street, New York, New York 10014, USA
Penguin Group (Canada), 90 Eglinton Avenue East, Suite 700, Toronto, Ontario M4P 2Y3, Canada
(a division of Pearson Penguin Canada Inc.)
Penguin Books Ltd., 80 Strand, London WC2R 0RL, England
Penguin Group Ireland, 25 St. Stephen's Green, Dublin 2, Ireland (a division of Penguin Books Ltd.)
Penguin Group (Australia), 250 Camberwell Road, Camberwell, Victoria 3124, Australia
(a division of Pearson Australia Group Pty. Ltd.)
Penguin Books India Pvt. Ltd., 11 Community Centre, Panchsheel Park, New Delhi—110 017, India
Penguin Group (NZ), 67 Apollo Drive, Rosedale, North Shore, 0745, Auckland, New Zealand
(a division of Pearson New Zealand Ltd.)
Penguin Books (South Africa) (Pty.) Ltd., 24 Sturdee Avenue, Rosebank, Johannesburg 2196,
South Africa

Penguin Books Ltd., Registered Offices: 80 Strand, London WC2R 0RL, England

The publisher does not have any control over and does not assume any responsibility for author or third-party websites or their content.

PRINTING HISTORY
Berkley trade paperback edition / September 2007

Library of Congress Cataloging-in-Publication Data

Griffin, Lynne Reeves.
Negotiation generation : take back your parental authority without punishment / by
Lynne Reeves Griffin. — Berkley trade paperback ed.
    p.   cm.
Includes index.
ISBN 978-0-425-21701-6
1. Parenting. 2. Parent and child. 3. Authority. I. Title.

HQ755.8.G7453 2007
649'.64—dc22

2007004996

PRINTED IN THE UNITED STATES OF AMERICA

10 9 8 7 6 5 4 3 2 1

To Tom—
I wouldn't have missed the dance.

Tell me and I may forget. Show me and I may remember. Involve me and I will understand.

—ANONYMOUS

Contents

Acknowledgments

Writing a book is much like nurturing a child. It takes patience, hard work, and the support of loving family members, good friends, and generous teachers. I wish to thank all those who made this book possible.

Tom Griffin, my husband and business partner. Your loving encouragement and faith in me are a bright light in my life. Over the years, your enthusiastic response to my ideas and dreams has sustained me. No doubt, everything good that happens is because of you.

Caitlin Griffin, my dear daughter and fellow writer. Your careful edits and thoughtful feedback were a true gift. The limitless emotional support you offer me every day defines the word *friendship*.

Stephen Griffin, my sweet son and fellow storyteller. Your sense of humor and positive energy are a daily blessing. Your patience and willingness to help me at every turn defines the word *generous*.

Elisabeth Weed, my literary agent. Everyone should have an agent as smart, hard-working, and responsive. The minute I met you I knew you would get this book into the hands of parents eager to be more proactive. I am deeply grateful.

Christine Zika and Wendy McCurdy, my editors. Both of you believed in my message enough to shepherd my book through production with a positive attitude and strong advocacy. A huge thank-you goes out to all the members of the team at Berkley/Penguin.

Amy MacKinnon, Lisa Marnell, and Hannah Roveto; writers extraordinaire. I am honored to be part of our writers' group. Each of you is a gifted and altruistic writer. Every ounce of feedback you've shared has been valuable to me in one way or another. I've learned so much about living a literary life from the three of you.

To all the parents who shared the ups and downs of their parenting experiences with me; I am especially appreciative. Your honesty and genuine desire to love and nurture your children in proactive ways is humbling to me.

part one
Setting the Stage

1. Why Too Much Power Is a Dangerous Thing

Sam had the face of an angel. From the moment he was born, his striking appearance and cheerful nature endeared him to everyone. His parents, Ellie and Chris, created a world that revolved around Sam; they'd wanted a baby for so long. They fed him on demand. They let him sleep in their bed. They took him wherever they went. The sun rose and set on their beautiful baby boy. Every child should be so loved.

The lifestyle his parents created by pouring themselves into parenting worked until Sam was two. But increasingly, Sam tested his parents' rules, and Ellie and Chris found it hard to set limits on his mischievous behavior. Sam's good looks and sweet smile helped him get around the rules that seemed meant for everyone else. By the time he was three, others weren't finding his behavior cute anymore. Friends and relatives nicknamed him *Dennis the Menace*, a nickname that served only to further excuse his behavior.

"Boys will be boys," his dad said to more than a few people who began struggling with Sam's complete disregard for rules. In preschool, he looked right at his teacher and threw a toy at her. When she tried to explain why he couldn't throw things, he flashed his beautiful smile as he covered his ears shouting, "I'm not listening."

By five, Sam had been asked to leave three preschools because his aggressive behavior was deemed unmanageable. Ellie and Chris repeatedly tried the suggestions teachers, pediatricians, and friends gave them; nothing worked. Opposed to spanking, they tried time-outs but Sam refused to sit or trashed his room. They took away his toys to which he shouted, "Fine. I don't like Legos, anyway." The star chart with incentives worked for only one day. His parents pleaded with Sam to be a good boy and placed hope in the belief he'd outgrow this phase. And for a while, he seemed to.

Sam loved school. He was bright, observant, and a quick learner. His elementary teachers spoke highly of him and the promise he showed for writing and music. He was articulate and had much to contribute.

But by the time he was ten, claims about Sam's aggression resurfaced. This time, bullying other children was the common complaint. One suspension in fifth grade became two suspensions in sixth. He skipped school, and his grades began to spiral downward. Reports of disrespectful behavior were widespread.

By high school, Sam's love of learning was a distant memory. Sam no longer dreamed of college; his parents prayed he wouldn't kill himself with drugs and alcohol. He drove the car his parents gave him into a tree, but lived to joke about it. At seventeen, he was expelled from high school for bringing a weapon to school. Today, Sam is as handsome as ever, but he doesn't go to school or have a job, and he no longer has contact with his parents.

Parenting Now and Then

It didn't have to be that way for Sam and his parents. All along, Sam's engaging though persistent temperament coupled with his age-appropriate limit pushing was really quite predictable. At each stage of development, Sam needed clear boundaries and consistent follow-through yet was unable to find them. Instead, Sam's ability to push boundaries and disregard rules took him further away from the person he could have become.

All along, Ellie and Chris loved their son and had the best of intentions for parenting him. What they didn't have was a parenting approach to fit his age, his temperament, and his challenging behavior. They needed an approach that embraced the belief: If you can predict it, you can prevent it.

Unfortunately, Sam's story of unfulfilled promise is common, though considered tame compared to other stories making headlines today. In fact, every evening you tune in to the nightly news, you'll find a story that raises the questions: What's the matter with kids today? Where are their parents? A five-year-old girl was placed in handcuffs by police because she was beating up her kindergarten teacher. A ten-year-old baseball player hurt his disabled teammate so the team would be more likely to win the next game. A teenage boy killed his girlfriend's parents with a shotgun because he disagreed with her father over her curfew.

Why are children increasingly out of control? The answer is a plague of negotiable boundaries. The children and the families you hear about in these stories didn't suddenly find themselves the subject of a news report or TV talk show because of an isolated incident. The outrageous examples of bad behavior you see everywhere you turn are the result of years of permissiveness, which is flourishing like a virus.

Once upon a time, parents were parents and children were children. Limits were clear, adults were in charge. Then the pendulum swung the other way, and parents were told to "validate" their children's feelings, and to encourage them to use their "words." Parents found themselves negotiating everything from breakfast to bedtime. Is it any wonder today's parents feel depressed, demeaned, and downright confused about how to do their job?

Do you feel like you've entered the twilight zone of parenting as compared to previous generations? You have. A day doesn't go by that there isn't a new pressure to understand, or a new limit to be set. Cell phones, instant messaging, satellite radio, and the Internet. New rules for dating, driving, dancing, and all-night graduation parties. And don't forget more homework, more afterschool activities, and more college applications. Your parents didn't have these particular issues to parent through, which makes it tough to look to them for advice.

With all the benefits of communication technology and the age of information, there are also drawbacks. While cell phones keep us connected, the Internet keeps us informed, and television keeps us entertained, parents have more to do than ever. Uncharted territory means setting new rules, and then being involved enough in children's lives to enforce them.

Over the years, there has been a real blurring of boundaries between adults and children. Babies get earrings, five-year-olds get allowances, ten-year-olds have cell phones, sixteen-year-olds have their own cars. No longer do children have to wait for or earn privileges. And, of course, how many times have you heard, *"In my day, we did what we were told,"* or *"Kids today don't respect anyone or anything"*?

I wish the nostalgia for the respect given parents in days gone by was just that, but unfortunately it is the result of parents who are no longer the authority in their child's life, negotiating the big and the small.

Ted, the father of four teenage boys, has always shared his love of baseball with his sons. Hats, jackets, and tee shirts with Boston Red Sox logos are everywhere in Ted's home. It wasn't until Ted got a phone call from his youngest child's middle school that he saw the clothing in a new light. "I couldn't believe the principal called me at work. She told me to come get Innis because he was wearing a YAN-KEES SUCK tee shirt. The school has a ban on what she called 'disrespectful clothing.' I thought I told Innis not to wear that shirt to school."

Ted's situation highlights just how much popular culture has changed and how desensitized most teens and adults are to it. Language was once tamer and role models were predominantly our neighbors, teachers, and family friends. Now, language largely goes uncensored, and role models are more likely those from the worlds of music, television, or movie stars. Pop culture glorifies anything that pushes the envelope.

Negative influences are all around you, sometimes coming from well-intentioned people, encouraging your child to engage in behaviors that are disrespectful, destructive, and dangerous. The Associated Press reported in January 2006 that parents in a suburb of Cleveland, Ohio, were responsible for the cancellation of an assignment in health class. The assignment, given to high school freshmen, was to research Internet pornography and write about the detrimental effects pornography has on those who view it. The superintendent of schools said

> *The first step is to understand the importance of your influence on your child's life and how to maintain your power over it.*

the teacher's intentions were good, and he's not likely to face disciplinary action.

Parents need help navigating the rough and unfamiliar terrain. The first step is to understand the importance of your influence on your child's life and how to maintain your power over it.

Is Your Clock Ticking?

When I ask parents why they think they are unable to parent more effectively, the number one reason is lack of time. It does take time to parent well; on some level everyone knows this. To anticipate the issues, to prepare your child for difficult situations, to follow through on nonnegotiable limits, to heal the hurts, to motivate, to celebrate accomplishments: They all take time. I don't know any parent who says he has enough of that precious commodity.

Unfortunately, the conventional wisdom for raising children today is robbing you of precious time. Have you heard, "You have to expose your child to enrichment activities like painting and flute lessons; after all, how will your child learn what she's good at?" Or, "If your child isn't on the travel league for baseball when he's ten, he'll never make the high school team." The pressure to cram activity after activity into your weekly schedule has reached ridiculous proportions.

> *Unfortunately, the conventional wisdom for raising children today is robbing you of precious time.*

Polly gets up at 5:30 in the morning. After putting the finishing touches on a book report, she gets dressed and packs some food for the long day ahead. Polly's parents repeatedly nag her to get going. "Get up. Brush your teeth." After an hour where emotions are running high for both Polly and her parents, they leave the house at 6:30. Polly spends the early morning with twenty children and one adult eating breakfast and talking about the school day. During the day, she does her school work in three separate class-rooms under the direction of four different adults. At 4:00 P.M., Polly goes to gymnastics. After gymnastics, it's off to a piano lesson. She arrives home after her lesson and changes into comfortable clothes. The nighttime routine includes a new set of power struggles between Polly and her parents. "Sit down and eat." "Empty your backpack." "Get going on that homework." At 6:45 P.M., bedtime is only a dream. At 7:00, Polly finally sits down to begin her homework. Polly is seven years old.

Are you intimately familiar with the phrase *dine and dash*? Dashing here and driving there, skipping meals and getting your child to bed later and later each night may be how your week unfolds. A schedule like that is tough even for parents who are not holding down a paying job as well.

Survey after survey shows that not only is insufficient time a leading complaint of working parents, but so is the guilt they feel about the *kind* of time they spend with their children. When you come home after a long day of work-related pressures and your child is behaving in ways clearly unacceptable to you, do you set limits or look the other way?

Madeleine is a single mom working hard to juggle her job responsibilities along with raising her six-year-old daughter, Tess. "A night doesn't go by that I don't end up yelling at Tess. Even though every morning I vow, 'I won't yell at her today.' But from the time I pick her up from her afterschool program until I kiss her goodnight, she argues about everything. 'I don't want to eat that.' 'The water in the tub is too cold and those pajamas are too itchy.' 'I want you to sleep in my bed.' If I give her an inch, she takes a mile. I start off being kind and nice, trying to make everything perfect but by the end of the night, I lose it."

What Madeleine describes is a classic attempt to focus entirely on quality time because she feels she can't offer quantity time. In the process, it's all too tempting to overlook Tess's clear attempts to find the limits.

When Tess pushes the limit on mealtime, bathtime, and bed-time, what she needs is for her mother to make it clear what *is* negotiable and what is *not* negotiable. When Madeleine responds by ignoring misbehavior in an effort to keep the peace, Tess feels compelled to push another limit.

Clear and consistent boundaries are what children need and what parents find hard to create. I can give you this guarantee: The more you shy away from creating clear boundaries, the more discipline issues you will face.

Boundaries can be as concrete and simple as a highchair or carriage, and as abstract as earning a privilege after doing some yard work. Clear and consistent bound-aries are what children need and what parents find hard to create. I can give you this guarantee: The more you shy away from creating clear boundaries, the more discipline issues you will face.

What Happens When Children Have Too Much Power?

Ivy is the mother of four-year-old Evan and an education and train-ing coordinator for a large software company. According to Ivy, she works part-time for the software company and overtime to parent little Evan. "I have the ability to run trainings for hundreds of staff members and I can't get Evan to pick up a single truck when it's time to clean the playroom. I'm too embarrassed to have other mothers and their children over because Evan doesn't listen to a word I say."

Ivy is one of so many parents confessing to have little or no control over her child's behavior. With feelings of frustration running high and belief in their ability to control behavior at an all-time low, parents like Ivy are engaged in what I call "feel-bad parenting."

When you're with your child, do you feel inept or exhausted because every request is met with "You can't make me" or "I won't!"? And when you're not with your child, do you feel guilty because you're apart, or maybe secretly glad you are? The pressure on today's parent to be a good provider, a "Super Nanny," and at the same time a best friend puts parents in the proverbial no-win situation.

> *The pressure on today's parent to be a good provider, a "Super Nanny," and at the same time a best friend puts parents in the proverbial no-win situation.*

"I don't understand why he won't listen to me. His preschool teachers say he's an angel at school. What am I to think? Maybe he doesn't like me," says Ivy.

Sentiments like Ivy's are all too common. Previous generations didn't worry about whether their children liked them. Don't get me wrong; I'm all for my children liking me but I recognize that quite often they will not. Sometimes they won't like decisions I make in their best interests, and I'm certain they're less than pleased with the limits I follow through on.

In a recent study of discipline techniques used by parents, the top-ranking strategy, coming in at 90 percent, was explanations. How many times do we have to watch Charlie Brown cartoons to notice that Charlie and the *Peanuts* gang, along with every child, hear adult explanations much like Charlie hears his teacher: "Wah, wah, wah"?

Neither your child nor mine wants explanation after explanation. When a child is met with a lot of chatting, nattering, and blathering, he'll join in the negotiations. If you've got something to say, then your child's got something to say. If you're having a conversation about anything other than limits or rules, then back-and-forth interchanges are wonderful. But when your child is faced with requests or expectations that are supposedly not negotiable—the talking is over.

In a recent study of discipline techniques used by parents, the top-ranking strategy, coming in at 90 percent, was explanations. How many times do we have to watch Charlie Brown cartoons to notice that Charlie and the Peanuts gang, along with every child, hear adult explanations much like Charlie hears his teacher: "Wah, wah, wah"?

The result of being repeatedly faced with mixed messages, rules that change, oodles of discussion, and lots of opportunity to change how situations turn out, is an increase in self-focused or entitled behavior.

Five-year-old Anna asks her dad for a yogurt. Her father gives her strawberry. Anna says, "Daddy, I want peach!" Anna's dad says, "Sure." He gets her the peach and she says, after he opens it of course, "Daddy, I don't like *this* peach. I like the *other* peach." "We don't have the other peach, Anna. How about this peach or the strawberry? That's a good one." To which Anna replies, "I want the other peach, right now!" She throws the yogurt on the floor while Dad sighs and begins to clean it up.

Maybe you've been in a similar situation and you're thinking, How could he have known that giving Anna a choice would end in a yogurt disaster? But the dance between Anna and her father is actually predictable. She's five: Five-year-olds love to exert new-found independence. Temperament plays a big role here, too. Is Anna typically more persistent, more intense, or more sensitive? And then there's the high probability that Dad and Anna have danced to the same song many times before. If you can predict it, you can prevent it.

Temperament is explored in detail throughout this book. But

for now, it's important to know that the yogurt example shows us how it's-all-about-me thinking is taught. It's called precedent-setting parenting and it will surely create behavior that looks self-focused, out-of-control, demanding, and beyond what you'd expect to see given your child's age and temperament. Our parents called it "bratty behavior." But it's unfair to blame your child for behavior that *looks* entitled and spoiled. You gave your child a voice, so now

> *It's unfair to blame your child for behavior that looks entitled and spoiled. You gave your child a voice, so now she thinks she has a choice.*

she thinks she has a choice. Once again, you've got to know when your expectations are negotiable and when they simply aren't. More on changing entitled behavior later, I promise.

A second by-product of too much negotiation with your child is escalating behavior. When your child is looking for a limit—and your child *is* looking for one—and he doesn't find one, he will misbehave in bigger and bigger ways until he does.

Seven-year-old Mark is working with his mother in the garden planting bulbs. Mark tosses a bit of dirt in his mother's direction. His mother's response is, "Let's not throw the dirt, okay?" Mark's mother thought she imposed a clear limit. But Mark heard a question that made him think the expectation was negotiable. So, Mark threw more dirt, this time a bit closer to Mom. She said, "Mark, I said don't throw the dirt, okay?"

Mark's mother, now frustrated with him, tried using stronger language but the limit remained soft. Posing limits as questions and asking a child if a rule is okay with him is not a clear boundary. Mark's behavior will persist until a clear, firm limit helps him make the right choice about behavior.

You can probably guess what happened next: Mark threw the dirt directly at his mother. Only then did she become more forceful.

Mark was not met with a clear limit with appropriate follow-through the first or even second time he tested the boundary. Predictably his behavior escalated until a real limit was imposed.

Have you ever found yourself with dirt on your face? Every parent has tossed out a soft limit now and again, but the child who encounters soft limits on a consistent basis will routinely exhibit escalating behavior. This is your child's attempt to find your limits. Your child needs clear, nonnegotiable limits to make sense of the world around him. And though he may not verbally ask you for limits, I'm certain his behavior is crying out for them.

Deciding what is and what isn't negotiable along with making expectations clear to your child, is the very heart of parenting.

Deciding what is and what isn't negotiable along with making expectations clear to your child, is the very heart of parenting. The child who doesn't learn to respect that which is not negotiable will have great difficulty behaving; first, perhaps just at home, but later in the neighborhood, at school, and out in the community.

When a parent tells me her child has difficulty behaving more at home than at school, this is valuable information. Inherent in school are some very clear limits. If a child behaves well in one setting and not so well in another, it says a lot about the clarity of what is and is not negotiable in one place or the other.

Here is the bottom line: The child with too much power feels unsafe, insecure, and at times, even unloved.

Be careful, though: The child who is not finding clear, nonnegotiable limits at home may exhibit disruptive behavior in the school environment as well, as he begins pushing limits any place he can.

Here is the bottom line: The child with *too much* power feels unsafe, insecure, and at times, even unloved. When one child in your family has too much power and control over other family members, everyone is negatively affected. As dramatic as this may sound, the child without limits is a child at risk for behavioral issues. When your child is young, perhaps boundary pushing is nothing more than an annoyance. But when your child is older, the consequences of ongoing boundary pushing are much more severe, sometimes life altering. There are some decisions your child simply can't make. Assuming she can may be setting your whole family up for more negotiation than anyone is prepared to handle.

Parent or Friend?

On a bright spring morning, Nora takes her three children to the playground. When they arrive she says, "Let's play a little and then we can have lunch." Two of her children happily run off to play on the swings. Her middle child, Ben, says, "No, Mommy. I want to eat now! And I don't want to eat at this picnic table, I want that one," he says, pointing to an occupied picnic table where other mothers have begun to stare.

"But there are other people at that table, Ben. I think we'll eat here, okay? Now, eat your PB and J and some grapes and then you can have your cookies." Ben, stomping and yelling, says, "I don't like peanut butter. I want my grapes and cookies now!" Nora quietly starts to play *Let's Make a Deal*. "Ben, just have three bites and then you can have the cookies, okay?" At which point Ben hurls the sandwich at Nora and throws himself to the ground, howling louder than a pack of wolves.

So, you've heard of baby boomers and you've heard of Generation X. But have you heard of Generation N? Could you be part of the Negotiation Generation? You might be if you find yourself in Nora's shoes hour after hour, day after day.

Many parents like Nora put enormous energy into parenting,

taking their role quite seriously. Yet this age of parents as friends has brought us to a place where limits are soft, boundaries unclear, and negotiations are taking place at every turn.

One reason for this generation of parents as negotiators is the age at which parents begin having children. According to recent census data, the average age at which an American woman has her first child has reached an all-time high of twenty-five years old.

So, you've heard of baby boom-ers and you've heard of Genera-tion X. But have you heard of Generation N? Could you be part of the Negotiation Generation?

This is because of a drop in teenagers having babies and an increase in the number of women having their first child during their thir-ties and forties. Why does this translate into more negotiation in parenting? The older you are when you first experience parent-hood, the more time you've spent concerned, first and foremost, with your own needs. Older first-time parents have spent more time in the work world and have spent more time negotiating the complexities of adult relationships, which certainly have different nuances than the parent-child relationship.

Older parents have enjoyed more leisure time, without the responsibilities of parenting. This may all add up to a rude awaken-ing of enormous proportions. Creating boundaries, setting limits and following through can be even more difficult for the parent who has experienced greater independence prior to having a child.

Hank, a first-time father at forty says, "Why can't we take our two-year-old son out to dinner on a Friday night? So, he runs around a little and maybe tomorrow he'll be a little cranky, big deal. Why should I have to make the sacrifice to stay home? And how will he learn to behave in a restaurant if we never expect him to learn?"

Hank said the dirty little word—*sacrifice*; perhaps the most uni-versal element of parenting across generations. Making sacrifices for your child has always been part of good parenting and it always will be. It's just part of the job description.

As a parent, you are called upon to put your child's well-being ahead of your own. I'm not talking about being a doormat. I'm talking about respecting the fact that your child is not a little adult. I'm talking about putting your child in situations certain to be met with success, not met with a high likelihood of misbehavior. You'll find if you can respect your child for the child that he is, he'll be able—and willing—to respect you in return.

> *As a parent, you are called upon to put your child's well-being ahead of your own. I'm not talking about being a doormat. I'm talking about respecting the fact that your child is not a little adult. I'm talking about putting your child in situations certain to be met with success, not met with a high likelihood of misbehavior.*

The age of Hank's child is the answer to his questions. At the age of two, his child will behave poorly in the restaurant because he has neither the developmental capability nor the life experience needed to behave well. Hank's son wants his jammies and a story more than any restaurant experience Hank has to offer. And Hank has plenty of time in the future to teach the social ins and outs of going out to dinner.

It comes down to a choice. Would you prefer to create situations where your child can behave well, or to put him in a situation that gives him every opportunity to behave poorly, leading you to ask, "What do I do when he does *that*?"

Information Is Power—Unless There's Too Much of It

In the 1960s, when everyone gathered around to discuss what Dr. Spock had to say, a revolution began: the parenting information revolution. Prior to Dr. Spock's sage advice, parents relied on their parents, grandparents, and neighbors for up-to-date information on parenting. Though professionals know so much about how children think and learn, most have yet to successfully translate that research into practical, everyday ways to parent. Parents tell me they struggle with having the right behavioral expectations, and struggle even more with the conflicting advice they get.

The popular approaches of the past focused on punishment, which leaves a child either fearful of future punishment or angry and resentful toward authority. Discipline today is weighted heavily on the side of talking and negotiating boundaries, which gives a child more power to make behavioral decisions than she is ready for.

Traditional experts often tell you to use time-outs for your younger child and grounding for your older child. But few parents find success with these techniques. Most parents tell me time-outs typically create new issues to negotiate. "Sit in that chair." "No! You can't make me!" And how about grounding? Today, when you send your teenager to her room, it's a wonder she doesn't send you a thank-you note. With TVs, iPods, and Internet access bedside, don't you wish your teenager would send *you* to her room?

Some experts say, "Encourage your child to use his words." But most parents claim one of the biggest issues they face is dealing with back talk. Encouraging talking about nonnegotiable limits simply grooms your child to push more limits. So much so, that once he starts pushing, he's relentless until you finally give in. Do you feel powerless to stay in the game long enough to outlast your

Most parents tell me time-outs typically create new issues to negotiate. "Sit in that chair." "No! You can't make me!" And how about grounding? Today, when you send your teenager to her room, it's a wonder she doesn't send you a thank-you note. With TVs, iPods, and Internet access bedside, don't you wish your teenager would send you to her room?

persistent child? This goes for giving your child choices, too. Giving a persistent child choices in conflict will fuel the conflict, not put the fire out.

Consequences, taking away privileges, spanking, and naughty chairs. Perhaps it's been your experience that these and other means of strong-arming your child meet with success—when you follow through. But these techniques are negative and fear-based, and while they may extinguish a certain behavior for the moment, they teach your child nothing about how to behave differently in the future.

Or how about the more positive, yet equally ineffective, feeling-based approaches to discipline? Star charts, rewards, and incentives. I've rarely seen a child who will behave well in the heat of the moment because his smiley-face sticker is waiting in the wings. Parents put tremendous energy into star charts when they could be putting that energy into teaching their child how to behave differently. And do we really want to raise a generation of children who will only behave because there's something in it for them? I certainly won't advocate buying good behavior.

No time-outs, groundings, or spankings. No privileges to take away, no choices, no star charts, no rewards or bribes. What else is there to propose? What could I possibly offer you?

Fences.

Fences Come in All Shapes and Sizes

Fences is my metaphor for creating solid boundaries and expectations that focus on building skills for behaving well, not punishment. Creating fences will involve learning when to *talk* and when to *act*. You'll learn how to create age-appropriate boundaries with clear and specific strategies to use no matter what your child's age or temperament. You, too, will come to believe: *If you can predict it, you can prevent it.*

If you wanted to learn to speak a new language, say French, you would immerse yourself in all things French. You might take a class, listen to tapes, read some books, or visit a French-speaking country. You would study. You wouldn't expect to be fluent in French for quite some time and only after you'd worked at studying quite a bit. But when it comes to parenting, most parents assume it will just come naturally. You either get how to do it or you don't. This simply isn't true.

Parenting is learned. You begin to learn how to parent when you're a child, by watching how your parents parent, through babysitting and taking care of your brothers and sisters. If those experiences were positive ones, you were fortunate. But if those experiences were negative or hurtful, what your role models taught you was ineffective parenting. You can't expect to know how to parent well if you've never been taught. But you can learn now.

You need a simple plan, one that you can rely on no matter what your childhood was or was not. You need a plan that will stand the test of time and new research. You need fences.

There are three factors that shape your parenting experience: your parenting style, which determines how you create fences; your child's style or temperament, which affects the way your child accepts certain fences. Let's face it, some children have more difficulty accepting limits and this book will help you plan accordingly. The third factor is your lifestyle, which, if more adult-driven than child-friendly, will make your child's behavior simply more challenging than it ever needs to be.

Examining these three factors and making simple, practical changes to all three will help you make unnecessary negotiation a thing of the past. You'll step out of the Negotiation Generation and back into control.

Stuck in the Middle with You

For parents the pendulum keeps on swinging. I won't suggest it go back toward the so-called "good old days," when parents ruled and children kept quiet. I won't suggest it swing toward a place where children are happy at all cost to the rest of the family, including the parents. What I will suggest is a mid-level position where parents are parents and children are encouraged and allowed to be children. Where parents are in charge and children respect this. Where parents know the difference between conversation and negotiation. Where children know what is negotiable and what is not negotiable. When the pendulum falls right in the middle, children will behave because it's the right thing to do—not out of fear or for reward, but because it's the natural, easy thing to do. Let me show you how.

2. Boundaries Help Everyone Behave

Come with me on a trip to the grocery store. Nina is heading straight to the deli counter to pick up some meat and cheese for a family lunch. When she arrives, she makes a beeline for the red ticket dispenser. She pulls her little pink ticket out; she is number 18. As she glances up to the number above, 15, she's able to gauge how long her wait will be. Nina browses through breads, trusting that her position is secure: 16, 17. She's next. Like the other deli customers, Nina waits patiently.

Then Nina hears, "Nineteen."

"Oh, wait I'm number eighteen. I'm next," she says. Nina's little pink ticket confirms her rightful place in line. She shows her ticket to the woman filling orders. Once validated that she is indeed next, Nina crumples up her little pink ticket and deposits it in the wicker wastebasket. No one at the deli counter challenges Nina's place in line. Her little pink ticket is a fence.

With little pink tickets for everyone, the customers at the deli counter behave. The system of tickets makes the process clear. You take a ticket; you wait your turn. Your number creates structure and fulfills your expectation. Your ticket allows you to relax because you're clear on how this will work. The system is predictable. Others around you follow the same expectations keeping the process orderly, fair, and stress-free. Once in a while someone will come to the counter and try to jump in. But the rest of the customers feel confident to say, "You need a ticket."

Now come with me on a different day to the grocery store. You head to the deli counter. You go to grab your little pink ticket out of the red dispenser, but it's empty. It's Saturday at noon and the deli counter is swamped. Now, if you're the kind of person who wants your order filled and will do what it takes to get it, you'll jockey for position in front of the counter. You may knowingly cut the line; after all you're in a rush. It's chaos, but you're focused on getting the job done.

Or perhaps you're the kind of person who hates confrontation, so you're the one everyone cuts. You don't feel comfortable with this free-for-all. You may even forego ordering, instead grabbing a quick-pick ham and cheese so you can get the heck out of there. Without little pink tickets, even grown-ups "misbehave." The expectations and process are unclear. Without structure or clear boundaries, customers' individual temperaments start to surface. People may or may not push literally but they are certainly pushing figuratively.

The Grass Isn't Always Greener

With boundaries clear and predictable, both adults and children behave. Without boundaries, life becomes unruly. Consider the aftermath of any type of natural disaster. At first, people are immobilized by fear and because of this they naturally gravitate to those who assume authority. If no one steps up to assume authority, and expectations for behavior remain unclear, civil unrest and issues like looting become commonplace. Perhaps only a few people take necessities like milk and bread to feed their families but then others follow suit. There is a domino effect.

One person pushes a clear boundary, in this case stealing. Then another person joins in and another, and so it goes. Once a critical mass is reached, people begin doing things that under ordinary circumstances would be seen as a boundary, or unacceptable; suddenly it becomes acceptable.

On a much smaller scale, this domino effect of boundary pushing happens every day, everywhere. I remember when I had a substitute teacher in third grade. The class risk-taker sent the first spitball in the poor replacement's direction but after the third or fourth child joined in, it was all-out warfare. If you're a parent of more than one child, you know exactly what domino effect behavior looks like. One child takes a cookie; then every child wants a cookie. You let one child stay up to watch a special television program and then every child wants the same.

If you take the time to look, you'll see boundaries all around intended to curb the domino effect. There are speed limit signs positioned by the side of the road, posted signs telling you when you can expect the doors to open at the library, and elaborate queues at Disney World that guide the waiting. Have you ever seen people behave so nicely in a line they've been standing in for over an hour?

Boundaries are valuable. Boundaries are vital. And everyone needs them. Creating them is fundamental to effective parenting. When you have them, they remind you of the perfect backyard.

Imagine the perfect backyard. Inside it there are great things to play with: swings, slides, and a sandbox for little children; a volleyball net, croquet set, and a basketball hoop for older children. Around that backyard is a solid fence. All the slats are intact and in place. There is a solid gate with a functioning latch. There are no holes for the dog to crawl under and it's just high enough to keep the children from hurdling over it. This backyard represents freedom *within* structure. If your child was presented with this backyard, he would play in it. Your child would be safe and secure as he explored his independence. And he would know he was expected to stay within the yard, while being free to enjoy all there was to do there.

> *Boundaries are valuable. Boundaries are vital. And everyone needs them. Creating them is fundamental to effective parenting. When you have them, they remind you of the perfect backyard.*

Now imagine another backyard. It, too, contains fun things to play with. But this fence has missing slats. Its gate is easy to open; in fact, the latch is visibly broken. There's a huge hole that the dog has dug, so that he along with anyone else can leave the yard at will. The visible hole and the missing slats are inviting your child to think, "What's on the other side of the fence?"

Even though this backyard has the same things to play with as the first, if presented with it your child would be hard-pressed to resist the temptation to leave. The holes in the fence attract attention and if one child explores this lack of structure, more will follow her lead.

The domino effect.

This backyard represents freedom *without* structure; your child simply can't function at her best in this kind of environment.

Boundaries and limits mean the same thing: a line, real or imagined that clarifies which behavior is acceptable and which is not. Boundaries, in turn, create individual physical and emotional safety zones.

Physical boundaries include which places you can go, how you will keep your body safe, and when you need to eat and sleep. Emotional boundaries include learning how to protect your feelings, who is best to befriend, and how you will respect the belongings of those around you.

Your child isn't born knowing his physical and emotional boundaries. These boundaries are learned throughout a lifetime and in a variety of ways. But first and foremost it will be you who teaches your child these and other important boundaries.

As a parent, you build fences everyday. When you insist your child eat her breakfast, you're teaching her that healthy bodies need good food to function well. When you separate brothers and sisters who are name-calling, you teach your children everyone deserves to be treated kindly.

Some of your fences will be new and well-built, while others may be shaky and in desperate need of repair. Your goal will be to build the new while you reinforce the old, until your child has a strong sense of these boundaries all on his own.

Some adults perceive limits and boundaries as confining or restrictive and thus negative. Certainly there are restrictive types of discipline like spanking and time-outs, which rarely change behavior in the long run. But excessive talking is equally ineffective and leads to an equally negative environment for you and your child. Didn't the customers at the deli do better when they had their little pink tickets?

It would've been fruitless to have someone standing at the counter saying, "Take a ticket, okay? Did you take a ticket? Why won't you take a ticket?" Adults wouldn't like all this talking; why do we think children will? This tactic often cements a person's resolve not to respond to the talking at all. It is with clear boundaries and certain action that accepting fences becomes easier to do.

In a suburb of Boston, a two-year-old was hit and killed by a car.

He refused to hold his mother's hand and ran into traffic. A client of mine, Penny, confided in me, "I could have been that mother. My four-year-old, Nick, refuses to hold my hand when it's time to cross the street at the busy intersection near his preschool."

She admits, she sometimes lets him run to the light and other times she tries to hold him back. She's tried pleading her case. "Crossing is dangerous. Nick, it's time to hold hands. Please hold

> *Boundaries and limits mean the same thing: a line, real or imagined that clarifies which behavior is acceptable and which is not.*

my hand, Nick. Take my hand now!" But Nick refuses and every day there's a scene at the crosswalk.

Penny believes Nick is old enough to know better and can make the choice to do what's right, he simply chooses not to. Penny keeps negotiating that which is not negotiable, so Nick sees holding hands as optional.

After you've given a clear direction to your child—the talking is over. Instead of constant negotiation every time Penny and Nick come to the crosswalk, she should simply take his hand. He will soon learn that holding her hand while crossing the street is a non-negotiable safety limit.

Are you, like Penny, concerned that setting limits and following through will in some way thwart your child's independence and decision-making? No need to worry. Remember, creating good fences means making it clear to your child exactly *what is* negotiable along with *what is not*. Rather than box your child in, I will show you quite specifically the freedoms you can create within the structure of your own backyard.

Penny was able to put up a new fence by making it clear to Nick, long before they got to the crosswalk, what she expected. Before leaving for school the next morning she said, "We can walk with your friends and you can press the button for the WALK signal but when we get to the light you will hold my hand. When we get there, I will take your hand without talking, because this isn't up for discussion."

When she got to the light that afternoon she found Nick resisting, pushing the new fence. In the past, Penny would try to talk her way through this fence pushing, making the limit negotiable. This time, she did not talk. She'd already done the talking. Now, she needed to act, to show him the rule was real. She took hold of his hand and marched across the street.

Nick was surprised at first. He resisted twice before he realized that holding hands wasn't negotiable. Soon he concentrated more on what he could do, than on what he couldn't do. Today, Nick holds his mother's hand without thinking twice about it.

Some critics of firm limits and boundaries claim fences actually encourage testing of limits. Contrary to this popular opinion, your child doesn't misbehave because he knows and understands exactly where the fences are and chooses to ignore them. He simply sees the fence gate open and he walks right out of the yard. In fact, try to see your child's misbehavior as saying nothing more than, "Where's the fence?"

Your job is to build good fences, all the while being prepared to routinely show your child where the fence begins and where it ends.

> *In the past, Penny would try to talk her way through this fence pushing, making the limit negotiable. This time, she did not talk. She'd already done the talking. Now, she needed to act, to show him the rule was real. She took hold of his hand and marched across the street.*

Clearly some children push fences more than others, and this reality will be explored in detail later. Your role in creating fences comes first. You must decide what fences matter most to you and how you will reinforce those aimed at safety or family harmony.

Some nonnegotiable expectations are obvious. Your infant must be buckled in his car seat. Your eight-year-old must wear her helmet when she rides her bike. Your teenager must have a license to drive a car. For most parents these fences are black and white, causing little difficulty in making rules become real.

Unfortunately, there are hundreds of decisions to be made every day that are shades of gray. Can my child handle a play date? Should my child have a cell phone? Can my child handle the advanced math course? Should I let my child hang out at the mall? These are trickier boundaries to establish—and trickier fences to build.

> *Your child doesn't misbehave because he knows and understands exactly where the fences are and chooses to ignore them. He simply sees the fence gate open.*

Creating a physically and emotionally healthy world for your child requires you to be *definite* about *all* of your fences. The way you create fences depends on your parenting style and how much your child pushes the boundaries you create. But if your expectations for behavior are unclear, then you're giving your child control over issues he is too young or inexperienced to consider. You are the parent and you must be the first to determine what to expect of your child physically, emotionally, socially, behaviorally, and spiritually.

Building Good Fences

You've created a fence when you convey to your child he must *wear a coat in winter*. Yet you convey the freedom within the backyard when you give your child the freedom to choose *which coat he will wear in winter*. Now, not all parents will agree that wearing a coat in winter should even be a fence. I live in New England and have a teenage son, so I can assure you nonnegotiable coat wearing isn't the most popular fence around town.

It's up to you to decide which fences to build. You may not care one way or the other whether your child wears a coat in winter. After all, you might trust that your son will put on a coat when he's cold. Or maybe your son has had frostbite in the past and you feel strongly about coats in winter, in which case you'll find a way to reinforce your fence.

Whether your child cleans his room once a week, once a month, or once a year is truly your business. How you will go about choosing which fences to build will depend on your values, along with what you think you can realistically follow through on.

Throughout the following chapters, I'll offer suggestions about the fences that are best. Drawing on my expertise in child development and temperament, I'll have strong suggestions about the fences I believe increase the likelihood your child will grow up to be a cooperative, capable, responsible, and respectful adult. Ultimately, however, the fences you choose to build will reflect your priorities and values. The fences you build will be vast. They fall into two categories: safety fences and respect fences.

Safety fences include rules for planes, trains, and automobiles. There will be fences for using the stove, surfing the Internet, and riding in cars with boys. There will be fences for going on field trips, visiting friends for the weekend, and going off to college.

Ten-year-old Olivia has been begging for weeks to be allowed to ride her bike four streets away to a friend's house. Her mother decides it's time to build a fence. She sits down with Olivia and says, "You can ride over to your friend's house today. When you get to her house you'll need to call me so I know you've arrived safely. If you're willing to do that, you can go."

Olivia, eager to accept the new fence, seemed to understand she could go if she called when she got there. Olivia's mother went on to build a very solid fence when she said, "You'll need to work hard to remember to call me. If you forget the first time, I'll call you. If you forget the next time, I'll have to come and get you."

Olivia's mother recognized her daughter's eagerness to accept the fence was because she wanted to go. She would have agreed to just about anything. But Olivia's mother also recognized her daughter was young, inexperienced, and likely to forget the rule. Or maybe she anticipated that Olivia would push the fence, to see if the limit was real.

Regardless of how or why the fence might get pushed, Olivia's mother must be prepared to make the fence real; she mustn't let Olivia through the figurative gate. After all, for Olivia's mother, this is a safety fence.

Respect fences include all the expectations you have for the way your child treats himself and others, including you. Teaching respect is an active process that begins with believing that respect is a right, not a privilege. It includes teaching your child that his behavior has the power to impact everyone around him in both positive and negative ways.

Sixteen-year-old Spencer is lively and chatty according to everyone who knows him. Yet he seems to have only two words in his vocabulary when talking to his dad: *yup* and *nope*. Spencer's dad says, "It's becoming increasingly difficult to talk to Spencer. Other parents of teenagers tell me it's just the way it is. Teenage boys get quiet and it's like pulling teeth to get one to talk. But do I have to put up with this phase? It just seems so disrespectful."

While you're certain to come across developmentally expected behavior as you parent, it doesn't mean certain behavior is acceptable or that you should tolerate it. And since you can predict it, you can prevent it.

No matter what the media or other parents tell you, believe

this: You *will* get the respect you expect. And I'll bust another myth here, too. Teenagers aren't disrespectful by nature. Just as respect is taught, so too, is disrespect. Sometimes your child simply can't find your respect fences anywhere he turns. Spencer's dad needs to create respect fences, regardless of Spencer's age, gender, or what other parents are telling him. Of course, he'll have to find ways to follow through on his nonnegotiable fences, especially if Spencer pushes them.

Both Olivia's and Spencer's parents were able to make safety and respect rules real in a very short period of time by creating fences in advance and following through consistently. So whether it's time to address no talk, long talks, or back talk, the rules you enforce are powerful forces for changing behavior. You too, can create safety and respect fences to help manage the behavioral issues that surface as you parent. While it's clearly easier to build fences when your child is young, it's never too late.

How Big Is Your Backyard?

The structure and boundaries you provide are the fences, and they're not negotiable. It is the freedoms your child has within that structure that are negotiable. Perhaps the fence at bedtime is that your son sleeps in his own bed but once in it, he can choose to read or listen to music. Or perhaps the fence for homework is that your daughter must do it before dinner but when she does, she can choose where she sits and which subject she'll work on first.

Becoming clear about your fences and your freedoms requires you to be proactive. You need to step back and examine where your child would benefit from a fence and what the backyard should look like.

When your child is young, the backyard should be small with fewer freedoms. A young child has difficulty when the backyard is too big and the fence is hard to find. With clear fences and few freedoms, your child will behave better.

Tony knows that when he takes three-year-old Maria to the mall today, he'll need a stroller. "The last time I took Maria to the mall, she went nuts. I was chasing her up and down the mall and finally threw her over my shoulder and left. I was so mad because she was laughing at me and I didn't even get what I came for. I will never do that again."

> *The structure and boundaries you provide are the fences, and they're not negotiable. It is the freedoms your child has within that structure that are negotiable.*

When Maria was faced with the enormous backyard of the whole mall, she was hard-pressed to find the fence. She ran and she laughed as she explored her freedom without structure. She had no idea her fence pushing was frustrating or perhaps danger-ous, and the fact that she seemed to enjoy her fence pushing was a major source of aggravation for Tony. Yet this scene was really quite predictable. Maria didn't go to the mall certain about the safe and respectful behavior expected of her. She could run, so she ran. She could lead because Tony followed. She didn't know where the fence was so she literally ran the length of the mall to find it. Three-year-old Maria required a much smaller backyard to be successful.

Before Tony's next trip to the mall he told Maria, "When we get to the mall, you'll be in the stroller. You can bring your dolly and a snack. You'll be able to get out when it's safe and only if I say so. If you don't want to hold my hand, you'll go back in the stroller. After my two errands, we'll get some lunch." On this trip, they finished the errands quickly and had time to stop at the pet store window.

It's important to create age-appropriate backyards. Tony read-justed the size of the backyard not to punish Maria, but because now he knows that with clearer expectations and a much smaller backyard, it will be easier for Maria to behave better. Given this smaller backyard, Maria was clear about what was expected, so she accepted her fence and was perfectly happy. Wouldn't you rather put the time into creating a backyard just the right size rather than find yourself in a situation where the yard is too big?

While you might be thinking it would be nice to keep your child in a stroller until she's safely deposited into adulthood, you know you can't. As your child grows, you *slowly* let the fence expand and provide your child with more independence. The backyard should get bigger and there should be more freedoms within the structure.

Unfortunately, there are two fairly common boundary issues related to fences for the older child. The first, and most widespread fence problem, is when parents, hypnotized by a child's indepen-dence, take down too many fences. Then when their child mis-behaves they react by throwing up fences, making the backyard feel restrictive and too small to their child.

Twelve-year-old Barney loves video games. He's had one game system or another since he was six. He plays alone or with his friends, morning, noon, and night. When Barney's parents see his latest report card, both the grades and the comments from his teachers confirm what Barney's parents have been thinking: Barney is not paying attention to his schoolwork. And he hasn't been for a while. In a heated discussion about the importance of schoolwork, Barney's parents take away all his video games. They tell Barney he can have them back when his grades improve. Barney is outraged. After all, he had free reign on the games and now he has none. He says, "What do the games have to do with school anyway? I'll do better, I promise. Just don't take my games."

Barney went from having no fence to having one that's too restricting. Barney feels he can't move without hitting the boundary. The *take away* of his games is a punishment. Though you could argue that the games are a big distraction to doing schoolwork, Barney is right: The *take away* of the games won't change his ability to do the schoolwork.

Barney needs two fences: one fence for his games *and* one fence for his schoolwork. Certainly taking away the privilege to play video games when he should be doing his homework is the right response at homework time. But taking away his games as a punishment won't change his ability to do schoolwork. In this case, taking away one does not guarantee success with the other. And not having a fence and then reactively putting one up will only make your child confused and angry. You don't want to wait until your child fails before you create the backyard that will lead to success. The goal of creating the right backyard for your older child is not to punish him for making poor choices but to guide him to make the right choices.

This leads us to the second common fence problem experienced by the older child and her parents. Some parents create backyards that are too small and are reluctant to slowly expand the backyard to include new age-appropriate freedoms. It's called being overprotective. With all that your child is exposed to in today's pop culture, it's tempting to keep the backyard small and fences tight. But your older child will exhibit troublesome behavior if the backyard is too small. If the fence is impeding independence and feels restrictive, she will rebel.

Sixteen-year-old Coco loves fashion. She reads the latest fashion magazines and loves to shop. Coco's mother only allows her daughter to buy clothes when she's present and she has strict rules about what Coco can and can't wear. To her knowledge, Coco respects the fence related to clothes, even though she grumbles and complains the rules are far too strict. One day when Coco's mother drives past the high school, to her shock she sees a girl who looks an awful lot like Coco wearing a very short skirt, a strapless top, and plenty of makeup. Coco jumped the fence.

There is a delicate balance between a backyard that is too small and one that is too big. It involves knowing when to talk and when to act. It requires thinking about fences proactively and being willing to modify them over time. And when you do need to readjust the size of the backyard, you do so because it's the right thing to do for your child, not in an effort to punish. Again, if your child is young, the backyard is small and the freedoms few. If your child is older, the backyard is bigger and there's more freedom. At each developmental stage, you'll need to revisit the size of the yard and its contents. But you never remove the fence entirely.

Now imagine the fences you currently provide for your child. The key to creating a balance between expecting too little of your child and expecting too much is understanding age-appropriate behavior and expectations. Do you have fences for mealtime, bedtime, and playtime? How about fences for homework, chores, and friendships?

You can find respectful ways of providing fences for your child for these day-to-day experiences. If you feel overwhelmed because you see so many fences that need to be built, start small by choosing one. Perhaps the morning routine is stressful; start there. Think about what structures would make it easier for your child to know what you expect. Be sure to factor in your child's age and temperament so the backyard you create has a sturdy fence and includes age-appropriate freedom.

Please Fence Me In!

Start with your nonnegotiable limits. Do you know what they are? You need to, because ambivalence is the enemy of effective parenting. If you aren't clear on your nonnegotiable safety and respect rules, you have a hole in your

Ambivalence is the enemy of effective parenting.

fence. And if there's a hole, your child will find it. It isn't easy to build nice sturdy fences all the time but when you do, your child will feel safe, secure, respected, and will be respectful. And you'll feel better about your parenting experience, too.

Today, you may decide to build a fence for teaching your child to ride a bike. You'll coach and encourage your child to ride without his training wheels. You'll run beside him, holding on until you're certain he has the balance and confidence to ride alone. If he falls off—and he inevitably will—you won't punish. You knew he would fall, so you'll help him get back on to try again.

Much of parenting is like teaching your child to ride his bike. It takes planning. It takes the right attitude. It takes perseverance. It takes patience. And it should always include giving your child the chance to make a mistake without being punished for it. Your child deserves to be picked up and given the chance to try again.

Robert Fulgham wrote a lovely book about the beauty of limits called *Everything I Need to Know I Learned in Kindergarten*. His list of rules includes: *Clean up your own mess, Don't take things that aren't yours*, and my favorite, *Play fair*. In parenting, the only way to play fair is to share the rules for living before your child starts to play the game. Create fences in advance. Let your child know where the fences are. And then, by all means, make sure the freedom within the structure is fun. With the right backyard, everyone can learn to play fair.

part two
Your Style

3. Three Factors That Shape Your Parenting Experience

On a warm sunny day in June, Owen mounts his horse and heads out to the far reaches of his property. His cattle ranch, in southwest Montana, is on the western slope of the Rocky Mountains. He rides through some of the most scenic meadows and hills in this part of the country. His aim, while moving the cattle, is to get to the fences surrounding his vast acreage.

His pace is set by the terrain and the respect he has for his horse, and the cattle, as he guides the animals to their new pasture. His is a journey, not a race. With baling wire and tools in tow, Owen examines the fences built to allow the cattle to freely roam the pasture while still staying within the confines of the property. When he finds a hole in the fence, he isn't angry and he doesn't ignore the hole he finds. He simply does what it takes to repair the breech in the fence, making it stronger than it was before, only to move along to the next fence, to the next hole.

The number of holes that need mending has everything to do

with how the fence was first built as well as how it's been maintained. Were the original materials strong enough and well planted in the soil? Are the fences capable of doing the job they were intended to do?

Owen's fences were not built to imprison. And the fences you build in parenting shouldn't be for that purpose either. Like Owen's, yours should act as a border between the places where freedom begins and where freedom ends.

Owen's fences were not built to imprison. And the fences you build in parenting shouldn't be for that purpose either. Like Owen's, yours should act as a border between the places where freedom begins and where freedom ends.

Three Factors

The concept of the fence is a concrete and simple one: The fence itself represents the nonnegotiable rules, while the negotiable aspects of life with your child are represented by the freedom within the backyard. Do you like this idea but feel overwhelmed with how many fences you need to build, or are uncertain where to begin building them? Sit back and relax. I promise to walk you through the process.

Your parenting experience is impacted by how you create boundaries, how your child accepts them, and by the way your family life is structured. Like Owen, you will want to build strong fences, reinforce them when necessary, and maintain them regardless of all the other things you could spend your time doing.

There are three factors that greatly influence whether your parenting experience is a positive or a negative one: your parenting style, your child's behavioral style, and your lifestyle.

When it comes to parenting style, every parent has a predominant way of responding to behavior. Do you wait until your child misbehaves, think to yourself, "What do I do now?" and then react in dramatic ways, trying to stop misbehavior? Or would you describe the way you respond to your child's behavior as inconsistent, one day certain of what you expect of him and the next day not so sure?

While every parent can have a reactive day or a wishy-washy moment, most parents have a primary and fairly predictable way of responding to behavior. Maybe you always react or waver, or

> *There are three factors that greatly influence whether your parenting experience is a positive or a negative one: your parenting style, your child's behavioral style, and your lifestyle.*

maybe your style is one where you anticipate the challenges of the day and plan accordingly. I have no doubt being proactive decreases stress and increases the likelihood your child will accept your fences. Your style has a great deal to do with how you parent and sets the stage for how your child will respond to you, both positively and negatively.

Since parenting involves a complex relationship, your child's way of responding to you is another important part of the equation. Each child is hardwired with certain predicable patterns of responding to his environment. If your child doesn't adapt well to change or needs clear expectations for how to behave and you tend to waver, the way you create fences is at odds with what your child needs. The same is true if your child tends to be impulsive and you tend to be reactive.

Do you feel you *are* consistent with fences, offer predictable, age-appropriate routines and provide clear nonnegotiables, and still have a child who has difficulty accepting your limits? It's possible you're already a proactive parent but your child is hardwired to have difficulty accepting fences. Given your child's temperament and your family's lifestyle, you may find more conflict in family life than you can tolerate. As you learn which of these three factors most impacts your parenting, you'll be able to make decisions about exactly which ones would benefit from some fine-tuning.

So Who's to Blame?

Let's be honest. You can't resist staring at the mother struggling with her child in the grocery store. Have you ever exchanged a judging glance with another shopper or felt you knew exactly how she should have done things differently? Or maybe you've delighted in watching the parenting reality shows depicting families in constant turmoil with uncontrollable children and thought, "At least I'm not as bad a parent as he is."

Face it, it's easy to blame a parent for the child running amok, especially when the hosts of such programs look right into the camera and roll their eyes at the very parents they've been called in to help. Blaming parents is hardly a new phenomenon; the blame game has been played forever. But today, it's out of control. Parents are blamed for pushing too much and not pushing enough. They're blamed for being uninvolved in their child's education and for being overinvolved. Go online to any search engine, plug in "blame the parents," and you'll find parents to blame for everything from the crisis of disrespect, to childhood obesity, to college graduates not being able to find jobs. You'll even find a television show in the UK called, not surprisingly, *Blame the Parents*.

Though it's really quite easy to take this simplistic view of placing blame on parents for children behaving badly, it doesn't begin to capture the unique set of challenges each family faces, making parenting the toughest job there is.

Janie sits in the waiting area of the local pharmacy staring blankly at the latest issue of a parenting magazine. Three-year-old Robby and five-year-old Katie are bickering loudly over the limited selection of children's books. Another customer, also waiting, can't help but notice Janie does little to curb the children's escalating behavior. When she can't stand another minute of the almost violent exchange between the two children she intervenes. "Excuse me, can't you stop them? They're about to tear each other's hair out."

Janie looks up from her magazine with tears in her eyes and says, "I'm sorry. I knew this wasn't the best time of day to bring them here because I know they're hungry and tired. But my husband needs these new prescriptions and this was the only time I had a nurse to stay and take care of him. I couldn't leave them home alone with him."

> *Go online to any search engine, plug in "blame the parents," and you'll find parents to blame for everything from the crisis of disrespect, to childhood obesity, to college graduates not being able to find jobs. You'll even find a television show in the UK called, not surprisingly,* Blame the Parents.

What had looked to another like a mother completely disinterested in parenting was really a mother overwhelmed by her responsibilities. Do Janie's children lack fences? Yes. Does she have children with styles of behaving that require more problem-solving skills? Yes. Is her lifestyle more focused on the adults in the family than the children? Perhaps. But blaming Janie will not help her make the necessary changes to her style, her children's behavioral style, or her lifestyle. Her parenting experience is much more than meets the judgmental eye of those around her. Blaming her isn't going to help her, the children, or you.

Putting an End to the Blame Game

Most people haven't had the luxury of seeing the beauty of an iceberg up close. Though what is visible is quite beautiful, only about one-eighth of an iceberg is above water. The true magnitude of its shape and features are near impossible to surmise by just looking at what's obvious; hence the expression *just the tip of the iceberg.*

I'd like you to think of every family, including yours, as an iceberg. What's visible to others—what's above the water—is your public behavior toward your child and his public behavior toward you. It includes your family's appearance, your community involvement, and may even include your ethnicity. Like the iceberg, much more about who you really are is below the surface. Others don't always know the thoughts and feelings you have about your child and parenting. You don't go around telling everyone you meet how your parents affected your parenting style. Your values, your religious beliefs, your relationships in private are all below the surface, and invisible to the people around you.

Throughout the following sections of this book, I'm going to delve deeply into each of the three factors that shape your parenting experience. You'll examine one style at a time using a quiz provided in each of the sections. When you learn more about what influences how you create fences and how you maintain them, you'll be able to choose the positive, not punitive, strategies you'd like to adopt.

I'll encourage you to see your parenting style, your child's behavioral style, and your lifestyle as neither right nor wrong, good nor bad, because it doesn't help you or your child if blame is the game you're playing. Instead, you can move past criticism and judgment of yourself and your child and recognize how easy it is to make positive change to each style. Let's agree to put an end to the blame game.

What Kind of Parent Are You?

The first factor you'll examine in detail will be your parenting style. The three ways parents typically respond to a child's behavior are in reactive ways, wavering ways, and proactive ways. Like many, you might think the wavering and reactive styles are bad and the proactive style is good. But I don't want you to think of these ways of responding to your child's behavior in terms of bad or good. Simply put, you'll see better behavior from your child if you build fences proactively rather than reactively or in wavering ways.

In order to move away from judging your parenting style, you'll need to understand it more fully. Regardless of which style best describes your parenting, you have strengths in parenting and I want you to recognize them. Once you do, you'll be able to build on them while you smooth out the aspects of your parenting style that are contributing to conflict in your family.

Take a moment now to examine your parenting style by taking the first quiz. I'm certain you'll find you're already proactive in some of the ways you interact with your child.

Are you a proactive parent?

– – –

You will be better able to focus your energies on learning how to be proactive if you explore the way you currently react to your child. Answer the following questions by circling the number that best corresponds to your initial reaction. At the end, total up all the circled answers to see how proactive you are in your parenting.

1-Rarely
2-Sometimes
3-Often

1. I show respect to my child by listening   1   2   3 ✓
   when she speaks.

2. I let my child make age-appropriate   1   2 ✓   3
   decisions.

3. I expect my child to be responsible
   and cooperative.
   1   2 ✓   3

4. I spend time with my child because I really
   enjoy his company.
   1   2   3 ✓

5. I take responsibility for teaching my child
   how to solve problems and manage stress.
   1   2   3 ✓

6. I ask my child to share her thoughts, ideas,
   and opinions.
   1   2   3 ✓

7. I encourage my child to appreciate and
   share his accomplishments.
   1   2   3 ✓

8. I talk to my child about my values and
   why they are important to me.
   1   2   3 ✓

9. I have a clear set of rules that everyone
   in the family understands.
   1   2 ✓   3

10. I keep requests and commands simple
    and direct.
    1   2 ✓   3

11. I respond to problems in ways that are
    predictable and consistent, and not based
    on my mood.
    1   2 ✓   3

12. I tell my child in advance what the
    results of certain actions will be.
    1   2 ✓   3

13. I am willing to hold firm to a request or
    expectation important to me, even if other
    families don't agree.
    1   2 ✓   3

14. I follow through on the limits I've set if my
    child disobeys or manipulates these rules.
    1   2 ✓   3

15. I make decisions counter to popular opinion
    when I know they are right for my child.
    1 2 ✓ 3

16. I anticipate situations in which my child
    might have difficulty coping with the
    influences of others.
    1 2 ✓ 3

17. I give my child concrete ways to say no
    to negative influences.
    1 2 3 ✓

18. I routinely help my child develop the skills
    she needs to deal with peer pressure.
    1 2 ✓ 3

19. I encourage my child to express his feelings
    about rules even though I may not change
    them.
    1 2 3 ✓

20. I express my love to my child every day
    by letting her know she always has a place
    to share her feelings.
    1 2 ✓ 3

Now add up your total number of points and see how proactive you are. Remember, even if you are a very reactive parent, you can become proactive. This quiz is intended to raise your awareness about what you're already doing well as well as highlight the areas you may want to focus on.

The Results

50–60 POINTS *The Proactive Parent*

If you scored between 50 and 60 points, you are a proactive parent. This means you see discipline as an important aspect of everyday parenting. In good times and bad, you teach your child the skills she needs to be successful in the world. Though you may have ups and downs in the parent/child relationship, your family life is generally harmonious. Keep up the good work, because every developmental phase will bring new challenges.

30–50 POINTS   *The Wavering Parent*

If you scored between 30 and 50 points, you are a wavering parent. This means sometimes you may be proactive yet other times reactive in your parenting style. My guess is that your child pushes fences because your expectations may be inconsistent and boundaries are unclear. You can become more proactive by focusing on the aspects of your parenting that are reactive and committing yourself to using more proactive strategies in those instances.

20–30 POINTS   *The Reactive Parent*

If you scored between 20 and 30 points, you are a reactive parent. You may feel that your home is full of conflict and family harmony is a myth. Take heart: Even the most reactive parent can learn how to be a proactive parent. You are taking the first step by reading this book. You can begin to be less reactive and more proactive starting now. Your child is worth the effort.

A Blueprint for Success

By now you've taken the quiz and gotten a more well-rounded view of how you interact with your child. Were you surprised at the style that best characterizes the way you parent or did it confirm what you already knew about how you respond to your child's behavior? Don't be surprised if at first you're more focused on the reactive or wavering ways in which you parent. It's human nature to be more focused on what you don't like about your own behavior than all the things you're doing right. You're probably harder on yourself than anyone else would ever be.

What I'd rather you do is keep your focus on your strengths. Perhaps you're a very loving parent, always being sure your child has a place to share his feelings. Or perhaps you're the type of parent who provides guidance in simple and direct ways. If so, keep doing these things. Then choose some other aspect of parenting you'd like to work on and focus your energies there.

> *It's human nature to be more focused on what you don't like about your own behavior than all the things you're doing right. You're probably harder on yourself than anyone else would ever be.*

In the following chapters, each parenting style will be examined. I'll describe why you might have a particular style, what it looks like in action, and the effect it has on your child's behavior. I'll show you how to move your style toward being more proactive because once you learn to anticipate behavior rather than react to it, your fences will go up more quickly and efficiently.

You might still be tempted to play the blame game thinking, "It can't just be my style that's making family life difficult." And you might be right. Remember, there are three factors impacting your parenting experience and you may need to make changes to any combination of the three to see less negotiation and more cooperation in your family.

You Can Change

Before taking the "Are You a Proactive Parent?" quiz, Beth was certain Lucas, her five-year-old son, was a challenging child. The morning routine in Beth's house was described as a nightmare. "I follow Lucas around all morning saying 'Get this, do that.' All while I'm trying to nurse the baby and get myself dressed so I can get Lucas to the bus stop on time. He knows what to do, he just doesn't listen."

What Beth realized after taking the quiz was that she doesn't really have a clear set of rules Lucas understands. When she says "Get dressed," four or five times, she's negotiating that which is supposedly not negotiable. If she *tells* him that many times, apparently he really doesn't have to do it the first time. She admits she hasn't told Lucas in advance what the results of his actions will be. Sometimes she dresses him; sometimes she yells at him. And when he's finally dressed, sometimes they make the bus and other times it's so late she has to drive him to school.

With her current morning routine, Beth's follow-through isn't consistent or predictable, so Lucas's behavior isn't likely to change. His behavior continues because Beth is responding to this problem in ways that are based on her mood and her stress.

By making changes to her style of parenting and moving away from her reactive morning routine, Beth saw big changes in a short time. One afternoon, she began creating her new fence for the next day's morning routine. When her baby was napping, Beth and Lucas enjoyed an afternoon snack while she talked to him about the way the following morning would look. "We have to work together to get to the bus on time. I will lay out your clothes the night before and I want you to get into them before you come down for breakfast. If you forget, I'll walk you back up. Then you'll eat while I feed the baby. When you're dressed and done eating, you can play. What would you like to play with while you wait for the bus?"

The first morning of the new routine, Beth did walk Lucas back up to get dressed. After all, what he expected, whether consciously or unconsciously, was that she'd remind him numerous times before he really needed to get dressed. She didn't talk; she simply walked and waited and he got dressed. Then it was on to breakfast, where she had to twice walk him away from the toys and back to his bagel. But on day one of the new fence, they made it to the bus on time. Small changes make a big difference.

In this situation, modifying Beth's style was all that was required. Lucas had been having difficulty with the morning routine because of the way Beth was creating her fences. When she changed her style, she changed Lucas's response to it. For some, finding success in parenting is as straightforward as that. For others, it will involve change on your child's part along with changes to your lifestyle.

Your Child Can Change, Too

Are you thinking: My child would never respond as quickly or easily as Lucas did? I challenge you to try first to modify your style and see what kind of difference it makes. Then if success eludes you, it will be time to examine how your child's style of behavior or temperament factors into your child's ability to accept your fences.

Matt drops Isabella off at preschool three mornings per week. She's had difficulty with dropoff from day one but it seems to be getting worse not better. Matt dreads seeing her cry and even though the teachers encourage him to leave and assure him she's fine once he does, he sticks around, trying to convince Isabella everything is okay.

When Matt took the quiz, he realized he anticipates Isabella's difficulty coping and he encourages her to express her feelings about how hard it is to separate. These are strengths in his parenting. But he also realized he does little to give Isabella ways to handle her feelings and has yet to teach her the skills she needs to separate more effectively.

In Matt's situation, he needed to create a fence for drop-off that included modifying his style while helping Isabella to modify hers. The day before the next drop-off, Matt prepared Isabella for how they'd separate. "Isabella, I know it's hard for both of us to say good-bye in the morning. I think when I stay, I make it a little harder for you to get started playing with your friends. Tomorrow, I'm going to bring you in and you'll pick the activity you want to start working on. I'll hug you and say, 'I love you, see you at three.' Then I'm going to work. You don't have to cry but if you do, that's okay. I'll still need to go to work. Let's practice what we'll do tomorrow."

Matt went on to share with Isabella other things she could do to feel better at drop-off: She could bring a special doll. She could pick her drop-off activity ahead of time. She could sit with her teacher, Miss Suzy, if she was feeling sad. Matt combined a change to his style with skill-building toward Isabella's style.

For a child whose temperament makes fences hard to accept, a parent is tempted to keep moving the fence. All those mornings Matt showed his reluctance to leave, he was teaching Isabella her concerns about staying were real. When he put up a fence and gave her the tools to learn to stay effectively, Isabella accepted the fence.

Are you interested in knowing how long it took for drop-off to go more smoothly? For Matt and Isabella, drop-off with a hug, an "I love you," and a smile happened in three days. In Part III, your child's behavioral style, along with the skill-building you can do to work toward her temperament, not against it, will be explored.

When Life Is Good, It's Great

Emily and Joseph have an active family life. They have demanding jobs requiring the whole family to travel and socialize with their business associates. Both parents love spending time hiking and biking with their four children—in short, doing any kind of physical activity that takes them outdoors. But Emily describes eleven-year-old April as the wrench in the family works. "I have four children; three are as easygoing as can be. They take life as life presents itself. And then there's April. She never likes the restaurants we go to. She complains she'd rather be in bed. She won't ski when we vacation in winter and she won't swim when we vacation in summer. We're an active, busy family and all she wants to do is sit and read. What's wrong with her and why doesn't she want to be part of this family?"

Emily and Joseph's family lifestyle may sound fun and exciting to you. But if your behavioral style is more like April's, you might be exhausted just hearing about it and really overwhelmed if you were expected to live it.

This situation describes a lifestyle that fits the majority of this family's members, but it doesn't fit April. Emily and Joseph's expectations for physical activity, socializing, nutrition, and sleep are mismatched to the rhythms of April's hard-wiring. You could say April doesn't fit into her family or you could say the family doesn't fit with April's style of living. Either way, it's neither right nor wrong—it just is what it is.

Given this family dynamic, Emily and Joseph will be required to make changes to the way they create lifestyle fences. They can prepare April for what she's required to do in those restaurants and how she'll need to speak with their business associates. Preparation in advance, with opportunities to practice will be essential to building fences for a lifestyle that fits all family members. But they will need to make some changes to their lifestyle, too, respecting April's need for a less active one.

Theirs is the most complex of parenting situations. While building fences, Emily and Joseph will need to balance helping April develop the skills she needs to accept some of the family's expectations along with making lifestyle changes that help April to be successful. It will be their greatest challenge to see April's needs and the rest of the family's wants and needs as different—not wrong, just different.

Is the Combination Locked or Unlocked?

Whatever combination of factors—your parenting style, your child's behavioral style, or your lifestyle—that require transformation, the key to change is to become proactive. The place where you have the most control over behavioral change is your response to your child's behavior. So, you'll start there, examining how to build fences and stop negotiating away your power to parent. This will be the first thing you'll do to take a step out of the Negotiation Generation and into a more proactive generation of parents.

> *The place where you have the most control over behavioral change is your response to your child's behavior. So, you'll start there, examining how to build fences and stop negotiating away your power to parent.*

Next, you'll examine how you can be a coach and guide, helping your child to accept the new fences you're committed to building. And finally, you'll take control over your lifestyle. You'll learn how to choose routines and focus expectations more on your child's development and unique temperament than on what others pressure you to do. Making these changes starts with you.

If It Happens Once, It's Once;
If It Happens Again, It's a Theme

4. The Proactive Parent

Mrs. Williams's first grade classroom is decorated with children's artwork and alphabet posters. Children's books cover every available surface. Apologizing for only being able to offer a miniature chair to Logan's mother, Julia, Mrs. Williams sits down with her for a parent-teacher conference. The goal of this midyear meeting is to discuss Logan's progress in learning to read and write.

Mrs. Williams begins by sharing how eager Logan is to learn to read and how he loves all kinds of books, especially ones about dinosaurs. Though common for his age, Logan is struggling with some letter reversals. He has difficulty with *b* and *d, m* and *n*.

Together, the women devise a plan that includes telling Logan what his strengths are for reading and writing successfully. They will also share with him what he needs to work on and how those goals will be achieved. More time will be spent showing Logan the difference between the pairs of letters he finds confusing. Looking at the letters, printing them, and reading books with a strong emphasis on the letters will all be part of the plan.

Neither parent nor teacher will scold Logan when he continues to reverse the letters, as they expect he will in the beginning. They know he'll require increased exposure, repeated practice, and patience until the time when he makes the connection and learning takes place. When the connection is made, they expect Logan will use the letters correctly.

These women—both of them Logan's teachers—won't pin his success on hoping he'll magically learn to use the letters correctly in reading and writing; they'll create a plan to jump-start his success. And they'll achieve it through positive active means, teaching the skills required to read and write well, not through punishment.

When it comes to reading and writing, parents and teachers recognize the need for a planned approach to learning. Don't you agree being proactive is essential to learning those complicated skills? Certainly there are children who can pick up a book and seemingly overnight know how to read it, but others need more coaching to experience the thrill that comes from first reading stories out loud.

Yet other behavioral skills are frequently seen in a different light, and they shouldn't be. If your child needs to learn to read, you teach your child to read. If your child needs to learn to stay in bed, you teach your child to stay in bed. To get along with his brothers, you teach him to get along. To finish her chores, you teach her how to finish her chores. The process of learning doesn't change because one skill is any different from another; the proactive parent knows this.

Power of Positive Role Models

Role models have the ability to inspire, motivate, and change behavior. These inspirational people have the power to influence lives. Sometimes they consciously use their power; other times, they're not even aware they have it. Some role models we choose and some just happen upon our path. Some role models use their influence wisely, while others squander it. Some don't even realize they have been cast in a role at all.

A role model is first and foremost a teacher. Whether you teach your child how to ride a bike, drive a car, or run a company, you're teaching by example. The words *parent* and *role model* are synonymous. If you're a proactive parent, you're a role model and you're constantly in a position to use your influence to inspire, motivate, and shape behavior. You are your child's first and most influential role model. Your child looks up to you, as he will later look up to a teacher. You're constantly explaining to him the rules for being successful, just as his baseball coach will later on. You're always showing him how to get the job done, as his boss will later on.

As your child grows, she'll be influenced by other role models like her dance teacher, her favorite movie star, or her college advisor, but you're lucky enough to get the job first. You have the power to set the stage for what your child believes a good role model should be. Positive role models—proactive parents—teach effective communication and problem-solving skills. They serve as mentor, advisor, counselor, teacher, guide, and tutor. Role models lead and when they do this well, others follow.

The Perfect Backyard

In every relationship there is a power dynamic. The proactive parent exerts her authority, strength, and force to *influence* behavior, not *control* it.

Thirteen-year-old Chloe is desperate to have a cell phone; after all, everyone else has one. Chloe's mother, Joan, agrees it's time to build a fence. Joan knows Chloe is ready because she acts responsibly with other family ground rules. Ever since Chloe began lobbying for a cell phone, Joan looked long and hard at how her daughter handled the land line. Chloe uses the home phone in small doses and doesn't monopolize the phone all evening. Her computer and Internet habits are reasonable and while she does spend time on teen websites, they're ones that have been approved by Joan in advance.

The way Chloe handles fences around phones and other technology gives Joan a lot of information about Chloe's readiness to handle the responsibility of a cell phone. Joan realizes Chloe will be using this phone with less supervision than any of the other technologies combined. She is going to make an informed decision.

Joan proposes a gradual introduction to a cell phone, starting with borrowing hers. "Chloe, I'm going to get a family phone. This phone will be kept by me and loaned out to you when you need it. You'll need to ask for it and you can start by using it to call me for a ride after basketball practice. If you use good judgment using the family phone, you'll have opportunities to use it more often. You'll need to leave the call history on the phone and return it to me after you borrow it. If you're not willing to adhere to these rules, you don't need to have this privilege."

> *In every relationship there is a power dynamic. The proactive parent exerts her authority, strength, and force to influence behavior, not control it.*

Chloe had imagined a very different backyard than the one Joan was proposing. Yet because Joan has been proactive about the fences for cell phones, sharing the rules for cell phone use *before* Chloe comes anywhere near a cell phone, believe it or not, conflict will remain low.

Even though Chloe may disagree with how this backyard looks initially, this is her opportunity to voice her concerns. As they talk, she realizes the backyard for using the cell phone *is* small, but she also realizes if she can accept this fence now, ultimately she'll have more freedom in the future. And since she wants a cell phone and this is how she's going to eventually get one, accepting this fence is a better option than not accepting it, and having no cell phone at all.

Practically Parenting

Proactive parents are born *and* made. Maybe you find being proactive instinctive, connecting easily with how your child thinks and learns. You might be able to predict with certainty what your child will do in certain situations. Your two-year-old son sees rocks on the beach; you know he's going to throw them. Your twelve-year-old daughter realizes the dishwasher is clean; you know she'll leave her dishes in the sink.

You don't wait until the cards have been dealt to see what hand you'll need to play; you stack the deck in your favor with a plan. Before your son picks up a rock, you bend down and tell him he can play with the sand and collect the shells but he needs to leave the rocks where they are. You'll tell your daughter if she finds a clean dishwasher you'll expect her to empty it and then put her dirty dishes in it.

The proactive parent's efforts to anticipate are frequently rewarded. By building fences in advance, sharing positive expectations for behavior, your child often does exactly what he's expected to do. However, if and when your child throws that rock or bypasses that dishwasher, the proactive parent doesn't get angry. After all, you predicted the behavior in the first place. The proactive parent follows through, putting rocks back on beaches while walking her two-year-old farther down the beach, or calling her twelve-year-old from her room to empty the dish-

> *The proactive parent sees conflict situations as opportunities for learning, not as arguments to win or controversies to avoid.*

washer. The proactive parent sees conflict situations as opportunities for learning, not as arguments to win or controversies to avoid.

Alyce, mother of five-year-old Lilly and seven-year-old Riley notices her girls are setting up to play the game Chutes and Ladders. Alyce knows Riley can be a competitive board game player and when matched with friends her same age, this is rarely an issue. But when paired with her younger sister, Lilly, who has her own competitive edge and less experience playing board games, the name of the game becomes playing to win instead of playing for fun.

In an upbeat manner, Alyce reviews her expectations with the girls before they begin playing the game. "Girls, you'll need to play by the rules on the box unless you both agree to make up new rules. If you do decide to make up new rules, first you'll need to take a break, agree on the new rules, and then go back to playing. If you can't agree on how to play, you'll need to use your words to explain what you're thinking but you're not to yell at each other. I'm more than happy to help you figure things out if you can't on your own. If you're not able to play like good sports, the game will be put away for today."

Playing a board game is good practice for learning how to be a good sport and on a day when the girls have been getting along, it's likely to go well. But on a day when the girls are less patient or more tired, playing a board game will predictably pose more of a challenge. Alyce is prepared for whichever way the situation will go. If the girls do well, after the game is over she'll point out specifically what each girl did to contribute to the success of the play. If either or both girls become overly competitive, Alyce won't ignore the behavior but she won't react angrily to it. First, she'll step in to guide the problem-solving and if the girls are unable to play without yelling, grabbing, or cheating—the talking is over. Alyce, without talking, will end the game.

Alyce is a parent who sees herself as a teacher. She takes responsibility for talking to her children about how to resolve conflict before it arises. Yet she also knows to step in with action—not talking—when her children bump up against a nonnegotiable fence. She's aware she'll need to show her children how to peaceably manage the typical skirmishes siblings experience.

Are you a natural when it comes to imagining the times and places your child will need you as a coach or teacher? Or do you have to work a bit harder to step back and try to foresee where and when a situation may get the better of your child?

Since skills for modifying your child's behavior can be taught; learning the skills to be a more proactive parent can be taught as well. You'll get better at predicting what your child is likely to do in any number of situations as you practice predicting. Regardless of your age or how ingrained less effective patterns of parenting may be, with a solid commitment and practical hands-on strategies, you can teach yourself to parent proactively.

Beautiful Fences or Beautiful Sheds

Proactive parents start by creating ground rules for potential trouble spots before they arise. Of course, it's important to be flexible and adaptable, and to know when to build new fences and when to repair old ones. Because fences are always up, your focus can be more on what your child is free to do within the backyard.

Expectations for behavior are centered mostly on what your child can do, not what she *can't* do. Family life is rich with structure, routine, and supervision. Bedtime, mealtime, and homework time all have a familiar look and feel. The proactive parent steps in with authority only when those clear fences are pushed. He finds ways to be there to reinforce them and make them real. While the proactive parent talks openly and honestly with his child in advance of conflict, when clear fences are ignored or manipulated, the talking is over.

It's Saturday morning and Joe, the father of four-year-old twin boys, is preparing to paint his backyard shed. He realizes caring for Abe and Noah while trying to accomplish his chore successfully is a long shot, but it'll be doomed from the start without a plan. He dresses the boys in old clothes. He gives each boy his own paintbrush, aluminum tray, and some simple directions.

"Boys, you can use your paint tray, not mine. And you can use your brushes on the shed. If you get sick of painting, you can play in the sandbox with your trucks or any of the toys I've left out in the yard. We will all be staying in the backyard this morning."

It would be tempting for Joe to get so deeply engrossed in his painting job that he overlooks the boys' behavior until they clearly and repeatedly push his fences. He could yell or plead with them to behave as he asked them to, but he would be talking about situations he's already declared nonnegotiable.

> *While the proactive parent talks openly and honestly with his child in advance of conflict, when clear fences are ignored or manipulated, the talking is over.*

Instead, Joe talks about a lot of things, but he doesn't keep harping on the rules. He keeps his focus on engaging the boys in the process of painting. They chat and laugh as they paint. Joe, all the while, redirects the boys' behavior with action. When Noah dips his brush into the paint can, Joe walks him back to his paint tray. When Abe begins painting the grass, Joe guides him back to the shed. And finally when it seems the painting experience is clearly too much for any of them to manage, especially Joe, painting time for the boys is over.

You've probably guessed Joe didn't finish painting his shed that Saturday morning. But in behavioral terms, the plan was a success. Joe made some progress on the shed and involved the boys up to a reasonable point. The morning remained pleasant and under control. Joe wasn't able to complete his paint job, but he was successful in teaching the boys to accept fences. *If you follow the rules, you may paint; if not, painting time is over.* Had Joe kept his focus on finishing the shed and not on the boys, it would've been a behavioral disaster—although one that may have resulted in a beautiful shed.

Parenting with a Plan

I love chocolate. If I come face to face with brownies, chocolate cake, or chocolate in any form, I know my diet will be in serious jeopardy. At a party, even on a day when I'm completely committed to healthy eating, I won't be able to resist the dessert table if I don't have a plan. My strategy might be to load up on low-calorie foods like salad and veggies, and simply stand far away from the dessert table. But I will not be successful if I simply go with my fingers crossed, especially if the chef is my sister and the dessert is her famous *pain au chocolat.* And I won't be successful depending on my friends to lecture or nag me. Likewise, your child needs a concrete strategy for dealing with difficult situations. A proactive parent anticipates predictable problems and goes in armed with a plan.

Nine-year-old Eric and his family are going out to dinner for his grandmother's eightieth birthday party. Debi, Eric's mother, is well aware of how the excitement will affect Eric's behavior. She knows the food will be served buffet style and Eric has difficulty making choices under pressure. She knows the restaurant is very noisy and Eric reacts with big emotions when he's overstimulated by loud noise, bright lights, and foreign smells. Thirty relatives will be attending, so she knows the social expectations for Eric will be high.

> *The proactive parent embraces the thinking,* If something happens once, it's once, if something happens again, it's a theme.

Debi realizes this outing could be a disaster for Eric and for everyone else in the family. She isn't going to wait until he blows up because they run out of his favorite dish or he can't sit next to his favorite cousin. She isn't going to wait until he refuses to give Grandma a big kiss right in front of relatives he hasn't seen in years. Debi anticipates Eric's potential difficulties and goes armed with a plan.

"Eric, you and I both know this party is going to be a lot of fun. But there are certain things you'll be expected to do, like kiss Grandma and speak nicely to all the relatives who want to chat with you. Let's talk about everything that will be fun and all the things that might be hard for you. Then we can come up with ways you can handle what you need to do and what you want to do."

You might wonder how Debi knew the party would be so challenging. Is it more your style to go to the party, get blindsided by Eric's behavior, and wonder, "How was I suppose to know he'd do that?" That's perfectly understandable the first time it happens. But remember Eric is nine; he's had difficulty at similar parties before. You are not reading this book because a problem came up once and never happened again. *If something happens once, it's once; if something happens again, it's a theme.*

Think about some of the themes in your child's behavior. What frustrates you? What frustrates your child? Does your child have difficulty behaving every time he goes to the grocery store, every time he plays with the neighbor's child, or every Saturday morning when it's time for soccer? Do these problems crop up at mealtime, at bathtime, or at bedtime? These are your themes in need of a plan.

The proactive parent doesn't hold on to the same ineffective plan expecting it will suddenly yield new or better results. Behavioral patterns or themes are recognizable, and new plans to shape more positive behavior can be developed. The power to change behavior begins with positive active language.

An Invitation to Behave

In my workshops, I like to ask for a volunteer from the audience, someone willing to do an exercise with me to illustrate the importance of positive active language and building fences. If you volunteer to assist me, I ask you to join me on stage and stand facing me. There's a chair behind where you're standing. The directions are simple: Just do what I tell you to do as I tell you to do it. Are you ready?

"Don't stand. Stop looking at me. Don't sit down. Stop looking at the audience. Don't turn to your right; don't turn to your left. No laughing."

As the exercise progresses, you're likely to feel flustered because you can't seem to choose the right thing to do, or to do anything right. Some volunteers laugh because they're embarrassed they can't seem to figure out exactly what I want them to do.

At first the directions seem simple enough, but the reason they're difficult to follow is because they're really a two-part exercise for your brain. First, you must figure out the opposite of what

I've asked you to do. Then you have to actually do this opposite action. There's no question about it: Whether you're a parent or a child, directions are clearer when phrased in the positive. "Sit down. Look at the audience. Stand up. Look at me. Turn left. Turn right."

If you're putting up a picket fence you don't need to use tools capable of building the Great Wall of China. Fences are best built using proper tools. The proactive parent uses positive words and phrases to convey exactly what a child can do; not those words focused only on what a child *can't* do.

Your son asks, "Mom, can I have a cookie?" To which you answer, "Yes, you may have a cookie after dinner." You didn't say no but your meaning was clear. Your fence was present but not limiting.

Your daughter asks, "Dad, can I borrow the car?" To which you answer, "Sure you can; I'll need ten dollars for gas." You didn't say she couldn't but your stipulation was clear. Your fence was present but not argumentative.

The fences are there; do you see them? But the emphasis is on the words *yes* and *you can*. The proactive parent concentrates on the freedom in the backyard yet fences are clear and present. If cooperation is what you want, you must be a role model for it. If you want a child who says yes, you must be a parent who says yes. The proactive parent knows when to talk using positive language and when matter-of-fact action speaks for itself. And quite often, the two must be combined to effectively teach, "I say what I mean and I mean what I say."

> *The proactive parent uses positive words and phrases to convey exactly what a child can do; not those words focused only on what a child can't do.*

Mike is an active three-year-old who finds it a real challenge to sit still long enough to eat his meals. Recently, he's gotten into the habit of using his hands to eat instead of using his utensils, and he frequently gets out of his chair. Before dinner his mother says, "Mike, at dinner you'll need to use your utensils for eating and you'll eat sitting in your chair. If you forget, I will remind you."

Now wouldn't parenting be easy if that's all it took to encourage Mike to use utensils and sit nicely in his chair? At the beginning of the meal, Mike is able to follow these simple directions; he uses his fork and he sits in his chair. But just minutes into the meal he picks up his chicken with his fingers; his mother hands him his fork. And when he gets out of his chair, his mother returns him to the table. Mike learns rather quickly, that to eat, he must follow the rules.

Are you wondering how many times Mike's mother needed to hand him a fork or walk him back to the table? Whether I tell you it was one time or one hundred times, it really doesn't matter. Consistency means always following through when a fence is pushed. I define consistency in parenting as doing whatever it takes.

Today, Mike may need his mother to hand him the fork four times; tomorrow perhaps only twice. But if his mother's fence is eating with utensils, then she will need to remind him every time he forgets. How long will it take for Mike to learn to accept this fence? Let's assume Mike's proactive mother remains consistent with her fences for eating; factor in Mike's age and his predictable patterns of responding to limits or temperament and you can bet he will learn to accept his mealtime fence within one to three meals.

If you want a child who says yes, you must be a parent who says yes. The proactive parent knows when to talk using positive language and when matter-of-fact action speaks for itself.

Is it possible that even with consistency, Mike might one day forget to use a fork while eating? Yes. What should his proactive parent do? She should hand him a fork.

Getting the Message

Knowing when to talk using positive language and when to act is characteristic of the proactive parent's style. Like a good school-teacher, directions are given in advance of a test of ability or skill. Routines are consistent and predictable. Expectations are age-appropriate and each child is held accountable for meeting certain standards.

Have you ever noticed the preschool child's typical day rarely changes? Your child orders his day around the very sameness of his preschool schedule. Your child takes pleasure in knowing exactly what will come next. He feels safe and secure knowing his teacher will carry out circle time the same way every day, lead the children out to the playground the same way every day, and prepare for snack time the same way every day.

Whether you're a child or an adult, you take comfort in order and routine. I teach a three-week parenting series and each week parents come, they sit in the same seats as the ones they chose the first night. I never assign the seating; they simply choose a seat and stick with it, as if a particular seat will keep them safe and facilitate learning. Because it does.

If a parent, with all his or her life experience, creates a comfort zone for learning by simply choosing the same seat each week, imagine how much your inexperienced child wants and needs the little things in life to be predictable. When fences are predictable, consistent, and clear, your readiness to learn is increased. And if or when they're pushed, fences stay put.

Susan is the mother of an eight-year-old girl and she's excited to be volunteering each Wednesday morning in her classroom. When she enters the classroom on her first day, she notices the children walking around the room, chatting with other students while the teacher, Mrs. Greer, is working with a small group of boys on reading. At first, Susan is surprised to see the casual atmosphere and that socializing isn't just allowed but encouraged. But as she settles into her task of organizing the day's craft project, she notices all the children are productive in their work, helpful to each other, and conducting themselves better than any group of twenty-five children she's ever seen.

She takes a closer look at Mrs. Greer's style. She's placed herself in the center of the action. When she notices a couple of children off task, she simply moves to where they are and with small action, redirects their efforts. She uses her fingertip to tap a paper and focus a boy's attention back on his page. She walks a girl to a quiet place to complete her writing work. And at one point, because the noise in the classroom has risen to a higher than acceptable level, Mrs. Greer walks to the light switch and shuts the lights off for a brief moment. Susan is amazed to hear silence fall over the classroom. The children know this nonverbal cue means "it's time to lower our voices." This classroom runs like a well-oiled machine because Mrs. Greer's built many fences in advance. And when a fence is pushed, and she knows they will be, she steps in with small actions reinforcing the fences necessary for everyone to learn.

Now, if Susan came into the classroom and it was chaos, with children talking and laughing but not getting anything accomplished, she wouldn't be happy. She knows children can't learn in an environment where expectations are unclear and follow-through is nonexistent. Susan would be even more alarmed if she found Mrs. Greer to be demanding, yelling and pleading with the children to follow her directions and get to work. Certainly some children have more difficulty learning and behaving, but Mrs. Greer's proactive style actively addresses this reality. And I will too, as we get into Part III on your child's fence-pushing behavior.

With fences shared in advance and reinforced when ignored, Mrs. Greer is very successful at teaching each child all he needs to learn. I don't know anyone who learns best in a chaotic environment or when yelled at or demeaned. Don't you believe all children need someone like Mrs. Greer? If you're like most parents, you expect and respect a teacher with a proactive style. And if you're a proactive parent, your style looks a lot like Mrs. Greer's. Your classroom is your home, your neighborhood, and your community.

The Long and the Short of It

The benefits of being a proactive parent can be measured two ways: short-term benefits and long-term results. The biggest short-term benefit is more family harmony. Though life still has its ups and downs and no family is perfect, day-to-day life is more positive than negative for the proactive parent. More often than not, your child does what you expect her to do, at home, with friends, and at school. Because you expect your child to be responsible and cooperative, you spend time with your child because you really enjoy her company.

Amy and her seventeen-year-old daughter, Molly, are shopping for a prom dress at a local mall on a Saturday afternoon. Amy has already shared with Molly her fences for post-prom fun. Amy's offered to have Molly, her boyfriend Victor, and her friends over for breakfast after the prom. At one in the morning, she and Molly's dad will drive her friends home.

"Mom, thanks for offering to do breakfast, but my friends would rather sleep over at Victor's. I know you'll probably say no, but I really want to be with my friends. Can't you reconsider?"

Amy doesn't get angry at Molly for trying to go back over previous discussions they've had about prom fences. She recognizes Molly's need to understand and embrace, if she ever fully can, why Amy has nonnegotiable rules. She's not negotiating that which is not negotiable because it isn't prom night; that's still a month away. And she doesn't plan on changing her mind. She encourages Molly to express her feelings about rules even though she will still require Molly to accept her fences.

"It must be hard to see the plans evolving into something you know Dad and I won't let you do. Boy-girl sleepovers aren't appropriate for seventeen- and eighteen-year-olds, Molly. Too much temptation and more than likely not enough supervision. I know you might not agree and that's fine. Do you want to talk about ways you can make your friends more interested in coming to our house? Which of your friends is likely to get a no from his or her parents? I'll do what I can to help you work within our limits."

Amy took responsibility for teaching her child how to solve this predictable problem and manage the stress that comes with it. At the same time, she made decisions counter to popular opinion because she knew they were right for her child, her family, and in keeping with her values. But creating the fence wasn't enough; she took the extra step necessary for helping Molly develop the skills she needs to deal with peer pressure and still accept the fence.

There's a time to talk and a time to stop talking. The proactive parent doesn't shy away from conversation as long as it's out of conflict. Amy talked with Molly a lot about her prom night dilemma, but on prom night the talking about alternate plans was over. And the proactive parent knows children of all ages need to talk about fences repeatedly in order to understand them, but that doesn't mean the fences are coming down.

The long-term results of this kind of talking—not in conflict and not with the intention of bringing fences down—is that something more powerful is being built. Fences built today build character for tomorrow. Knowing when to talk, when to listen, and when to act is what being proactive is all about.

Proactive parents provide their children with good role models so they can make good choices. Their self-esteem is intact so they take care of their bodies and their spirits. With clear boundaries, they're less likely to push limits, drink, smoke, or use drugs. Children with expectations that are just right manage stress, don't get depressed, perform well in school, and don't get into trouble. Children who feel respected respect others. Respectful children grow into respectful adults.

Expect Success

Whether you're already a proactive parent or you really want to be one, this style of parenting is the ideal style, the one every parent should strive for. Thinking like a teacher, the proactive parent understands a child's development. He factors in his child's unique temperament, fully aware of situations that pose challenges for behaving in acceptable ways.

Creating proactive plans that involve when to talk and when to act, the proactive parent builds fences and reinforces them, no matter how many times the strength of the fence is tested. When you parent with a proactive style of parenting, your child sees fences, accepts them, and ultimately learns to create his own. The discipline you provide at first is external but in time your child learns self-discipline, motivated from within to make good decisions regardless of the decisions of those around him.

Isn't that what every parent wants?

5. The Reactive Parent

As the summer sky turns shades of pink and orange, the Clarke family's annual beach party is already in full swing. Older children are riding the waves to shore, where younger children, covered head to toe in sand, are surrounded by colorful blankets, beach chairs, and sand toys. Four generations of adults and children have come together to enjoy good company and lively summer fun.

This year's game of tug-of-war will be between the adults and the children. The teams are positioned on either side of a pool of water created earlier in the day, lined with plastic, and filled with the saltwater hauled up just a few feet to where the sand is level.

The teenagers and younger children organize themselves, staggering left then right on one side of the rope while moms, dads, aunts, and uncles do the same on the opposite side. Like the size of most families, today's game has more children than adults in it.

When the whistle blows, the game begins. Parents pull; children pull harder. For every action in this game there is a reaction, each time the adults try to draw the children to their side, the children try desperately to do the same. Everyone is yelling, clenching their teeth, and grimacing. Competition is high, cooperation is low. The winners will be those who have the strength to keep the push-pull dynamic going the longest, not allowing themselves to be dragged to the other side. It's a battle for power and control. No one is willing to drop their end of the rope.

In parenting, as in tug-of-war, the rope represents a power play dynamic between the reactive parent and her child. Like the pulling and tugging in the game, daily life for the reactive parent is a series of actions and reactions; the child pushes and the parent pushes back. The reactive parent uses her strength to pull her child to her way of thinking and behaving while the child uses every ounce of strength to do the same. There are sides; competition is high and cooperation low. Yet in the game of tug-of-war for power and control in the reactive parent's family, there is no winner.

Anatomy of a Power Struggle

Power struggles occur between you and your child when one or the other of you exerts strength or force in an effort to control behavior. Though everyone's been in a power struggle before, the reactive parent plays this game often and well. The game may begin in response to a limit being set—a fence being built—but soon it becomes a predictable pattern of interacting, where no one gets his or her needs met.

Power struggles happen when you and your child don't agree on fences. Over time, this way of relating becomes automatic. You and your child put forward strenuous effort to see who will successfully gain power and control over the other person's actions. Yet sometimes the game's played just to win.

These highly charged emotional exchanges create frustration, anger, and resentment between you and your child. Bitterness becomes the basis for every discussion, causing further breakdown in communication until it seems all you do is argue with your child.

Like the game of tug-of-war, the objective centers on winning, with each person equally committed to doing so. And both easily lose sight of the initial fence.

> *The reactive parent has a fierce desire for control. Yet if you're fighting for control, you're fighting.*

Your child can't engage alone; you can't play tug-of-war without someone on the other side of the rope. How often do you pick up the rope? Do you need to win control at all cost? If so, then you're role modeling competition to your child, showing him it's important to be the winner. Does your definition of parental authority mean never dropping the rope? The reactive parent has a fierce desire for control. Yet if you're fighting for control, you're fighting.

At the End of Your Rope

The power dynamic in the relationship between the reactive parent and her child is centered on the ability to control. Since no one, in any relationship with another, appreciates being controlled, the reactive parent has little to no influence in changing her child's behavior.

Wyatt, an active, independent five-year-old is described by his mother, Sara, as someone who knows how to push her buttons. Sara would tell you she has a clear fence for the car: Wyatt must sit in his car seat, buckled, before the car is started. Yet every day, without fail, Wyatt and Sara struggle for power and control over this fence.

"First, I fight with him to get into the seat. Then to get it buckled. And when I finally do, I'll be driving and I'll look in my rearview mirror only to see he's unbuckled it and is looking right at me to see if I'm going to do anything about it. I've begged and I've pleaded. I've explained it's the law. I've even pulled into a police station to scare him into staying buckled. Finally, I end up yelling at him and forcing the buckle into the catch. I have to lose it before he actually gets in and stays in. I can't take it anymore."

Did you notice all the talking Sara did to try to get Wyatt to accept this fence? She begged and pleaded, explained and threatened. But it wasn't until she stopped talking and used the simple action of buckling the seat belt each and every time Wyatt unbuckled it that helped Wyatt realize this fence wasn't negotiable.

Part of what Sara found so infuriating about this situation was the way Wyatt looked her straight in the eye as he defied her rule. This is something called social referencing, and it is a developmental capability your child acquires as early as his first year of life. Your child will look to you in ambiguous circumstances in order to get clarifying information about whether a situation is safe or behavior acceptable. Simply put, when your child goes to do something and he looks you right in the eyes, what he's really asking is: Is this a fence? Social referencing drives the reactive parent crazy. It's important to resist seeing this as flagrant defiance. When Wyatt looks right at Sara, his behavior is saying nothing more than: If this is a fence, make it a fence. This is Sara's cue to follow through and make her rule real.

To change the reactive dynamic, Sara must tell Wyatt before they get in the car that he must wear his seat belt. If or when he unbuckles it, she needn't say any more about it. She needs to stop the car and rebuckle the seat belt, no matter how long it takes them to get to their destination. This is the action that will teach Wyatt wearing his seat belt isn't up for discussion.

I'll Get You, My Pretty

The reactive parent sees discipline as punishment. Behavior isn't something to be shaped, taught, or influenced; behavior is to be controlled. Fences tend to be built in the heat of the moment, and without warning. The reactive parent expects his child to accept fences at a moment's notice and takes personally the child's natural tendency to resist. Once the reactive parent sees or feels resistance, his reactions escalate, equaling more resistance. The reactive parent jumps to the only thing he thinks will control his child more fully: punishment, the ultimate control. Get him before he gets you.

Everyone remembers the childhood classic *The Wizard of Oz*. Dorothy, a mere child, lands in a foreign place and in a situation she isn't prepared for. Much to her surprise, she finds herself wearing beautiful shoes that don't belong to her. The Wicked Witch of the West, who desperately wants the shoes, never asks matter-of-factly for them. She never shares her feelings about needing or wanting the shoes. The witch does nothing but react. She threatens Dorothy; she yells at her, and frightens her. At one point, she banishes her to a room far away from her friends and family, away from everyone who loves her or anyone who might help her figure out how to solve her complex problem of returning to Kansas.

This reactive authority figure believes all along that Dorothy knows exactly what she's done wrong but simply chooses not to set things right. But Dorothy is a child in a situation she's never been in before. She perceives her only option is to take revenge against authority and to fight for her freedom. This conflict is ultimately the witch's undoing.

Fairy tales and classic stories bring to light universal struggles of childhood. Many of them depict how a child yearns for independence while at the same time faces the insecurity that comes from solving problems alone. Dorothy's story illustrates teaching and learning as a series of punishments, overreactions, and miscommunications. She's scolded and dealt with severely. Power struggles are everywhere and there's a heavy focus on adult and child being pitted against each other. Like most power struggles between an adult and a child, the ending to the story is negative, punitive, and the reactive participants are the ultimate losers.

I don't know anyone who deliberately chooses to be reactive. Quite often, the reactive parent was once in a position where the shoe was on the other foot.

Reacting for a Reason

Parenting skills are learned. Your own parents taught you a great deal about parenting in the ways they cared for you. Unaware you were being taught, the way your role models built fences and the way they followed through—or didn't—contributed to the development of your parenting style.

Blake is the father of four children ranging in age from two to ten years old. He describes being a reactive parent much the same way other parents talk about this parenting style.

"I don't want to yell at them. I think I've got a handle on my reactions to the kids' stuff they do and suddenly I blow. It's like all the times they haven't listened or done what I've asked them to do stack up until I finally lose it. What bothers me most is hearing myself say the same rotten things my father said to me."

Have you ever vowed you'd never say certain things to your child, things your parents said to you, only to hear the very words come out of your mouth in the heat of the moment? Even if you didn't care for the way you were parented, it's all too easy to repeat the cycle of reactive parenting that you grew up with.

Jenny, the mother of two little boys, begins to cry as she shares with me how much she detests her reactive style of parenting. "I don't like the fact that every day I feel like screaming or spanking the boys. Most of the time it's about silly little things but I just don't know how to handle them. Jamie won't take a nap or Oliver won't get his shoes on. Why do I find parenting so hard? It shouldn't be this hard."

As Jenny and I further explored why she reacts, she shared with me that her parents weren't present a good deal when she was growing up. Her dad worked long hours and her mom was emotionally distant, leaving Jenny's older sister the task of caring for Jenny. Like many parents with the reactive style, Jenny was never exposed to good parenting skills.

Unlike Blake, who had negative reactive role models, Jenny didn't have any parenting role models. Jenny wasn't taught how to parent by watching her own. She didn't see how the typical issues of childhood are managed. When she's in stressful situations or comes up against something related to development or temperament she's never experienced before, she reacts to her children's behavior in the moment without having created a plan to manage it.

Whether your parents had a rigid view of the parent-child dynamic, or were absent physically or emotionally, you might easily find yourself reacting more than you wish you would. Add in a stressful lifestyle, where you take each day as it comes, and you've got a recipe for reactive, ineffective parenting.

A Backyard Too Small for the Game

Reactive parents, like proactive parents, create ground rules for behaving in acceptable ways. In contrast, though, they create the rules as they go, not before predictable trouble spots arise. Described as inflexible and rigid, if you're a reactive parent you value the need for fences but your focus is more on the fence than what your child is free to do within the backyard.

Expectations for behavior are centered mostly on what your child *can't do*, not what she *can do*. And the reactive parent often has expectations for behavior that are developmentally too high, expecting a child to behave in certain ways simply because you said so. Challenging behavior far outweighs acceptable behavior because you think your child should do what you say, when you say it, leaving little room for your child to need you as a coach or guide. Little attention is paid to what an age-appropriate and respectful backyard should look like, because the focus is too heavily weighted on the strength of the fence. Your child is often presented with a stockade fence when a garden fence would do quite nicely.

Family life is very structured and supervision frequently too intense. Bedtime, mealtime, and homework time all have seemingly impossible expectations based on a lack of understanding of what is truly appropriate given a child's development and temperament.

The reactive parent steps in with authority even when a kind word or gesture would be enough to convey meaning and garner cooperation. Rules are reinforced with time-outs, take aways, and grounding. Emotions run high in the reactive family. Fences are accepted by your child out of fear of punishment, not because your child is internally motivated to behave well.

The reactive parent does far too much talking in conflict, making nonnegotiable rules ripe for a power struggle. Your child pushes fences to find them; yet when he does, you choose to react rather than teach, demanding fences be accepted. And when you use drastic methods to control rather than influence behavior, you've picked up your end of the rope.

On Saturday afternoons, Teddy, a very social nine-year-old,

loves to organize backyard baseball. His friends come from all over the neighborhood to join in the game. Teddy's mom, Haley, sees the boys coming and gets a sick feeling deep in her stomach.

"I hate seeing Teddy organizing this stupid game. Everyone argues over who's going to be on whose team. It takes them half the time to figure out what's fair. And for goodness sake, it's the same kids every weekend."

When finally the boys have negotiated teams and reviewed the rules, they begin to play. When the ball comes too close to the house, Haley shouts to the boys out the kitchen window to move the play farther into the yard. When the boys argue over a play at home plate, Haley shouts out once again, this time telling the boys to figure it out without arguing or the game will be over.

Teddy begins to feel the backyard getting smaller and smaller as Haley becomes more involved in the game. When two boys object to Teddy insisting he didn't strike out at bat, Haley marches outside and tells Teddy if he can't play fairly, he'll have to come inside. Teddy begins to react against his mother's struggle for control. "Mom, you don't know how to play. It was a ball, not a strike, and you weren't there to see it. I'm not coming in!"

Both Teddy and Haley have the rope in their hands. She pulls. "What did you say to me? Don't you talk to me like that. Come inside this instant."

Teddy pulls. "No, you can't make me. It's my turn and I'm taking my base."

Haley's behavior escalates. She storms over to Teddy but he starts to run away. The other boys look on as the game of baseball turns into another sort of game. If it weren't so sad and scary, it might look comical. As Haley chases and threatens, Teddy runs and resists. When she finally gets to him, she forces him into the house. Teddy begins to cry and apologize, now that he truly feels the fence in the form of his very angry and embarrassed mother.

The game is over. The fence was found. But the effort and energy it took to control rather than influence the events of the baseball game taught nothing about how to solve problems with friends. Teddy and the boys did not learn how to play backyard baseball well. Haley spent all her precious energy focused on what the boys couldn't do. Without a different, less reactive approach, next Saturday's game will likely look exactly the same. With fences too tight and no freedom within the backyard, it's just too hard to play baseball.

Since Haley knows the boys have this difficulty each time they play, it's a theme for her and Teddy. She can build fences for acceptable behavior before the boys arrive next Saturday and then she can supervise in ways that show the boys how to play fairly. When she chooses to do this, the next game will look and feel very different.

An Invitation to Misbehave

In an effort to keep fences up, the reactive parent uses strong negative language, often threatening punishment. The reactive parent lectures. Unfortunately, using language aimed at controlling your child does more to fuel power struggles and invites more misbehavior than it encourages your child to accept fences. When you say, "Oh, no you don't," your child's behavior will show, "Oh, yes I can." Do you see the rope? When you pick up the rope, your child is invited to do the same. If you're talking, the issue is still up for discussion.

Allie and her three-year-old, Gaby, decide it's a beautiful day for a walk in the neighborhood. Gaby insists on riding her tricycle while Allie walks alongside her. With no fences built before the walk begins, Gaby feels free to ride like the wind. But early in the walk, Allie sees potential dangers, so she builds fences as she goes. When Gaby rides in the middle of the street, Allie talks. "Gaby, get over to the side." When Allie gets nervous because Gaby is too far ahead, she talks. "Gaby wait for me. Stop, right there." But Gaby keeps on riding.

The walk continues this way, with Allie trying to build fences by talking, and Gaby riding free because she can. As her concerns grow and Gaby's behavior remains unchanged, Allie's frustration starts to rise. "Gaby, how many times have I told you? If you don't stay over to the side, we're going home."

Far too many times the reactive parent will talk, plead, and threaten before she steps in with small and appropriate action. Allie continues to send the message that this fence is still negotiable because she's still talking. What role does three-year-old Gaby play in this power struggle? Not a very big one. She didn't know the expectations in advance and she's not being coached to accept them now. Whether Gaby hears her mother or not is irrelevant; she doesn't feel the fence.

How long will the situation continue this way? It will depend on how far Gaby goes, how unsafe the situation becomes, and how short Allie's fuse is today.

If you struggle with the communication patterns characteristic of the reactive style, your language actually encourages your child to get into a power struggle with you. "Go ahead; do it one more time." "Don't you dare." These phrases, used often by the reactive parent, are a setup for a battle of wills.

In parenting, there's a time for talking and a time for action. The reactive parent has a timing problem. She begins building fences with far too much talking and she does it in conflict. "Pick that up." "Don't touch that." "Get over here." When a child doesn't respond to commands at a distance, and few children do, the reactive parent moves to build a stronger fence, this time with threats of punishment. "If you do that again, I'll———." "I'm taking away———." "Go to time-out." "You're grounded."

When threats of punishment don't work to influence behavior,

> *In parenting, there's a time for*
> *talking and a time for action.*
> *The reactive parent has a timing*
> *problem.*

the reactive parent starts to feel so many different emotions: frustration, anger, even disbelief her child won't do as he's told. The underlying reason for these intense feelings? Lack of control. And the reactive parent despises not having control. So what's the next move in this game? The reactive parent chooses language that diminishes her child. "Why can't you ever—" "You're driving me crazy." "I've had it with you!" And finally—if it hasn't happened already—the reactive parent yells.

No one enjoys being a reactive parent, though many parents claim yelling works. Do you find it's only when you lose it that your child finally starts paying attention to what you're saying? It might be your experience that yelling works but it's probably because along with yelling you finally took action.

Allie did yell at Gaby but she also took her home. *Action.* When you yell and *do* something else—turn off the TV, take a dinner plate, sit a child in the high chair, walk a child back to bed, take a toy, turn off the computer, put homework back in a backpack—and the list goes on—yes, you've yelled, but you've also taken action. What the reactive parent doesn't realize is, it's the action that delivered the message: This behavior is no longer negotiable. When you're in conflict, action, not talking, does the teaching.

There is one type of action, however, that should never be taken by a parent: spanking. Somewhere in the chain of events that leads to a loss of self-control by the reactive parent, physical methods of punishment may be tempting. Spanking is a reactive and very hurtful way of putting up fences. Advocates of spanking say it works as long as a parent uses it to teach a lesson and only when a parent is in control of his emotions. Yet the lesson you teach when you strike a child is fear, control, and dominance; it certainly doesn't teach a better way to behave in the future. And while some say spanking is effective when a parent is in control of his emotions, it is the rare parent that makes the choice to hurt a child when in control. Most reactive parents make this choice when frustration is high and more proactive and effective ways to influence behavior elude them. Whenever you take action with your child that involves moving him, carrying him, or removing him from harm, you should always do so respectfully and without hurting him physically.

If you're a reactive parent, you might frequently ask the question, What do I do when he does that? This question is a sure indicator you're waiting until your child pushes a fence before you decide it's time to teach. When you wait until the fence is pushed, you're already in conflict. When you're in conflict, actions speak louder than words. And both our words and actions send powerful messages about behavior.

Missing the Message

When the messages you give to your child repeatedly include the words *stop, don't, you can't do this,* and *you won't do that,* your child starts a desperate search for what he *can do.* Though this might look to the reactive parent like more fence pushing, it's merely an effort on your child's part to find the freedom within the backyard.

All day, in every way, your child tries to communicate his needs to you. If you're a reactive parent, your child learns his needs are something he must fight for. Have you ever heard the expression "Negative attention is better than no attention at all"? The game of tug-of-war you play with your child becomes the predominant way your child learns to relate to others. Negative, controlling language—the power struggle—becomes his way of connecting to you and later, to other people. This, he thinks, is how I get my parents' help, attention, and love.

Lindy, the mother of thirteen-year-old Carlos, has told him on a number of occasions he can't be home or at any of his friend's houses if a parent isn't there. It's school vacation and Carlos and his friends are roaming house to house playing video games, shooting hoops, and hanging out. Knowing her son is next door and assuming a parent is home, Lindy dashes to the supermarket.

When she returns, Carlos and his friends are in her den playing video games. In front of his friends she says, "Carlos, you know the rule. No friends inside when I'm not here. Everybody out."

Embarrassed, Carlos says under his breath, "Stupid rule. Let's go, guys." Lindy and Carlos start connecting the only way they know how; the struggle for power begins.

Lindy reacts. "What did you say to me? Boys, you can go. Carlos, you're staying here."

Carlos gets angry. "You can't tell me what to do. I'm thirteen and I can go and do whatever I want and you can't stop me."

"Oh, really," Lindy fights back. "Watch me. No more friends for the rest of the vacation. You're grounded. I'm sick of you not listening to me. Go to your room and don't come out until I tell you to."

The scene quickly goes from bad to worse, because this is the usual pattern of communication between Carlos and his mother. Without much provocation, Carlos becomes physical with Lindy and she reacts by calling the police. Their power struggle started over a simple fence—one Carlos disregarded, that's true, but one

Lindy clearly reacted to. When the police arrived and were able to bring the emotions down, Lindy calmly expressed why she was afraid of the boys being unsupervised in her home or any other.

"I worry the boys will be tempted to do things. You know, drink or smoke pot. I was young once and I know how it is. I love you, Carlos, and I want you to do the right thing."

Partly because emotions were back in check and partly because the police officer was skilled at mediating this type of conversation, Carlos was able to tell Lindy what he couldn't tell her before.

"We were at Joe's house, his mother wasn't there either, and the guys wanted to try his dad's beer. I said I wasn't gonna do it. And I got a bunch of the guys to come back over here."

When you react, you're focused so intently on the offending misbehavior you miss the good decisions your child is making. In Carlos's view, he tried to do the right thing and ended up getting in trouble anyway. He pushed one boundary to avoid pushing another more serious one. The reactive parent underestimates a child's need for an ally. Instead, she thinks of her child as the enemy, someone who's prepared to fight fences rather than accept them.

When you react, you pick up the rope, forcing your child to pick up his end of the rope and defend himself. And then the power struggle is on. Unfortunately, once the tug-of-war is in play, healthy communication is over. Power struggles rarely, if ever, lead to genuine conversations about true feelings, motives, needs, or desires. The reactive parent de-

> *When you react, you're focused so intently on the offending misbehavior you miss the good decisions your child is making.*

livers more negative messages, all about what her child can't do. Positive messages, or what a child can do, are left out of communication, which makes it harder and harder for a child to connect with others in healthy ways.

On the Ropes

Living with a reactive parent on a daily basis has both immediate and long-lasting effects on a child. The immediate effect of a reactive dynamic, or lots of power struggles, is a home filled with constant conflict and poor communication. Your child learns it's only when she pushes boundaries that she gains clarity about fences. She learns freedom must be taken since it isn't likely to be offered. She learns that parental attention is negative and suspicious. She learns that needs and desires in her family are communicated in loud, demanding, unrelenting, and in some cases, physical ways.

For the child who avoids conflict at all cost, needs and desires go underground, creating lifelong patterns of entering unfulfilling relationships. But for the child more likely to push fences, fences will be pushed. Unfortunately, the fence-pushing child of a reactive parent often feels that in order to get out from under parental control at home, she'll assert herself outside her reactive parent's scrutiny.

Fourteen-year-old Marilyn has always been described by her mother, Kate, as persistent. "She's just like me, which is why we get into it about everything. I know she'll push me but I know I'm going to win. After all, I'm the mother."

Kate describes herself as tough and strict; she keeps Marilyn under tight control at home. And while Marilyn seems to tow the line there, it's another matter entirely at school. Kate's been called into school for a conference with Marilyn's guidance counselor, who shares with her the significant concerns she has about Marilyn.

"I'm sure we both agree Marilyn is a smart girl capable of great things. But increasingly I'm concerned about her. She skipped school earlier this week, her grades aren't what they could be, and unfortunately we think she's having issues with drinking."

Kate's shock is quickly replaced with anger. "Wait until I get my hands on her. Marilyn knows this is unacceptable. I'm on her about her schoolwork and I have strict rules about drugs and alcohol. How can this be happening?"

Over time, the child of a reactive parent comes to believe in all the demeaning negative remarks made to her over seemingly little things; years of reactive discipline affects self-esteem. Learning acceptable behavior only through a series of punishments, power struggles, and heated exchanges, she never learns how to enjoy age-appropriate freedoms while making good choices. If Marilyn has only been taught to make decisions about behavior with Kate nearby to badger her, guilt her, and force her to do it Kate's way, how would Marilyn have learned to make good choices on her own? Like many teens today, Marilyn doesn't feel good about herself. In an effort to be accepted, she's likely to try anything so she'll fit in with friends and be accepted. She doesn't trust her own decision-making ability, which makes her highly susceptible to peer pressure.

> *Over time, the child of a reactive parent comes to believe in all the demeaning negative remarks made to her over seemingly little things; years of reactive discipline affects self-esteem.*

Drop the Rope

No one can play tug-of-war without someone on the other side. What would happen to the reactive dynamic in your family if you suddenly dropped the rope? When you let go of your end, no one can play. The struggle for power and control ends, because there isn't any resistance. Without resistance, your child can't play either, though he may try at first without you. But the struggle will end and conflict will be dramatically reduced. When conflict is reduced, only then are you presented with a real opportunity to parent more effectively.

If you want to learn how to drop the rope, you'll first need to recognize when you're in a power struggle: talking about that which is not negotiable. Once you recognize you're in one, the talking is over.

Build fences in advance of difficult situations so you won't have to do it as you go. Step back and think through how your child is likely to behave with friends or when you play together. Anticipating how situations will evolve is a valuable tool for any parent, yet it's a skill undervalued and underutilized by the reactive parent.

If you find yourself in a situation you were unable to predict or feel ill-prepared to manage, recover it the best way you can, without a lot of talking. Later, you can reflect on whether this was a one-time problem or represents a theme. If it is indicative of a theme, you'll be able to plan ahead for next time.

When you talk, choose positive language. Replace "Don't hit," with "Be gentle." Replace "Don't bite," with "Kiss only." Replace "Don't stand," with "Sit down." And most important, stop talking when you realize you're in conflict. Always use small action first. If you know you'll ultimately have to pick your child up, remove the unsafe object, or take your child out of a difficult situation, do so early in the process. Trust what you already know about your child. Cut to the chase, getting where you're going to land anyway—just do so more quickly and efficiently and without talking. Remember, action, not talking in conflict, teaches. While at first finding the appropriate actions might seem challenging, they're always there and they are always smaller than what you usually choose to do.

When you choose less reactive ways of creating fences, following through, and delivering messages about behavior, you'll be on your way to a more proactive way of teaching your child to accept your fences. Your child will learn to accept fences while still enjoying the freedom within the backyard. She'll learn how to respond to physical and emotional boundaries and still make good choices, at every age.

Do you want to know how not to pick up the rope in the first place? In chapter Seven, "Parenting with Style," you'll learn everything you need to know to parent less reactively. When you adopt a more proactive style, you'll enjoy more family harmony, your child will behave better, and you'll enjoy a deeper, richer relationship with your child. You'll want to spend time with her because you truly like her and have fun with her—and other people will feel the same way.

6. The Wavering Parent

A trip to the town library is a regular event for Greg and his four-year-old daughter, Emma. All week, both Greg and Emma look forward to spending Saturday morning together, choosing books, reading books, and looking for the right movie to watch later at home. Greg is excited to share in his love of reading with Emma, and encourages her to choose books about all the things they love to talk about: birds, rainforests, weather, and seasons. When their weekly visit is over, Emma is always eager to present her selections to the librarian for checkout.

When they first began visiting the library, Greg told his daughter she could choose three books and one movie. Emma asked for a fourth book and Greg, happy to see his daughter's enthusiasm for books, agreed. Several trips to the library later, Emma was requesting seven books and three movies. Once again Greg, seeing no harm, said why not?

Five months and a ten-book limit later, Emma continues to

challenge her book limit though she doesn't ask for more movies because the library has a three-movies-per-card maximum. Greg, once able to carry Emma's library loot home in his hands, is now contemplating buying a bigger book bag though he just bought her one a month ago.

Greg jokes that maybe he should go right to buying a bookmobile, since that's what it might take to satisfy Emma's desire for books, books, and more books.

Though Greg is thrilled with Emma's passion for reading, he realizes it's not practical to allow the number of books to continue to climb. Emma will need a reasonable limit to the number of books she can take out of the library. This Saturday before leaving home, Greg tells Emma they will stick to a ten-book, three-movie maximum. He tells Emma even if she finds another wonderful book after she's chosen her ten, she'll have to put one back to accept the new one and still only take ten books out of the library. Emma agrees to the plan.

Later, sitting on the floor at the library Emma lays out her choices and with the thoughtfulness one uses to choose anything of value, Emma picks ten books. She returns the others to the shelf. Placing the books carefully in her bag, she proudly carries her selections to the front desk.

Greg didn't need to extend the book limit any further and he didn't need a new book bag or a bookmobile—though who doesn't love a bookmobile? Greg needed a fence. And so did Emma.

Indecision Is a Decision

When Greg neglected to create a fence for Emma and her books, his lack of a decision *was* a decision. Without a fence for the library, Greg created an experience for Emma that became all about the number of books she could have and not about the experience of spending time together. In fact, Emma's continued requests weren't about books at all; they were about fences.

At first, Greg didn't have a strong need to limit the number of books Emma could choose; to him, this issue didn't need a fence. Yet, Emma was only able to accept the way the library visit would go with a predictable, immovable boundary. She literally and figuratively needed a limit. When he said the number was five, she took five. When he said the number was ten, she took ten. Without a clear decision on his part, Emma continued to ask for more, trying to find the fence. Notice she didn't ask for more movies; the library had established a clear limit there. Greg's indecisiveness led them down a road where Emma pushed and Greg, for quite a while, chose to keep changing his expectations. All along Emma looked to Greg for direction.

When you make a decision, you've chosen a road to travel. Regardless of the road you choose, with every decision you'll face a new set of issues or problems to solve. What most don't realize is the same is true when you *don't* make a decision. With every decision *not made* there comes a new set of issues and problems to solve, too. They're simply different issues and different problems.

Let's say you're traveling in a car and you choose to go east; this means you won't be going west. When you go east, you'll meet people and see things that will affect how you think, feel, and behave. On this eastbound road, there will be obstacles to getting where you're going, but at least you're on the road, moving in your chosen direction.

When you refuse to make a decision or neglect to make one, you've still chosen a road to follow. Unfortunately some of these roads are dead ends and others are rotaries; the decision you've made when you *don't* make a decision is to be stuck, right where you are.

While the road you choose when you make a decision isn't free of obstacles, the road of indecision is paved with lost opportunities and fear of making wrong choices. When you're indecisive, you'll have to contend with the results of choosing to travel a long distance without a map, a compass, or a plan. Unfortunately, without clear decisions—without direction—the parenting road will be a long and difficult journey for you and your child.

You're Not the Boss of Me

When you waver, the power dynamic between you and your child is neither one of influence or control—for you. When you waver about fences and inconsistently make them real and true, your child has all the power in your relationship.

Pammy, the mother of four-year-old John, is one of the most pleasant people you'll ever meet. With her friendly smile and accommodating ways, everyone who meets her loves her. But Pammy would tell you she doesn't think her son likes her, since he resists everything she does to parent him well.

"Bedtime is exhausting. John just won't sleep in his bed. I used to lie down with him but now he insists on sleeping on the couch while his dad and I watch television. Before we call it a night, we slip him into his bed. But not long after we do, he shows up in our bed and stays there for the rest of the night. I'm constantly trying to explain to him how important it is to get a good night's sleep and how much better it would be if he slept in his own bed. But every night it's the same thing. I tell him to stay in his bed and he comes out. I end up letting him do it his way because I know once he's made up his mind, I'm powerless to change it."

> *When you waver about fences and inconsistently make them real and true, your child has all the power in your relationship.*

Powerless. Pammy feels powerless, so she is powerless. But John has plenty of power. At four, he has the power to dictate where and when he'll sleep. He has his parents jumping through hoops to get him to sleep their way. But only John has the power to make up his mind and refuse to change it. Does a four-year-old have the ability to make this decision? Or perhaps the more accurate question is, should he?

The wavering parent sees her child's reach for power as normal and healthy and may often encourage her child's desire for control. After all, she thinks, adults want to be in control of what happens, why wouldn't her child feel the same way? But just because a child reaches for power and control doesn't mean he really wants it. Just because he expresses a desire for it doesn't mean he should be given all the power, all the time.

In this parent-child dynamic, John has power because Pammy has relinquished hers. While bedtime fences are very important and need to be clear, what's more concerning is the powerlessness Pammy feels over this ordinary parenting responsibility. If Pammy feels powerless to create and reinforce the fence for bedtime, how in the world will she be able to create fences later for higher-stakes behavioral issues?

Tied Up in Knots

The wavering parent sees discipline as negative, and conflict as something to be avoided if at all possible. She doesn't see behavior as something to be shaped the way the proactive parent does or controlled the way the reactive parent does. Rather, the wavering parent believes a child can be sweet-talked into behaving in acceptable ways. He believes the child can be won over to the parent's way of thinking with coaxing, convincing, and intellectual arguments aimed at explaining the benefit of doing what the parent wants him to do.

In these instances, clear boundaries are hard to find; since the wavering parent doesn't feel she needs them, why would her child? Yet when frustrated, the wavering parent expects her child to do what she says simply because she said so, frequently claiming her child is one who doesn't listen.

> *The wavering parent sees discipline as negative, and conflict as something to be avoided if at all possible.*

When she sees resistance to cooperate or an inability to accept one of the few fences that do go up, the wavering parent steps in with even more talking. She uses conflict as another opportunity to explain her point of view.

Like the rope that exists between the reactive parent and her child, a rope is present between the wavering parent and her child, too. Instead of the push-pull dynamic the reactive parent engages in, the wavering parent, along with all her explanations, holds on to the rope and lets her child drag her around by it. The child ends up with more power and control than is age-appropriate. Even with all the authority, your child isn't winning when he can negotiate non-negotiable behavior. When expectations are unclear, accountability nonexistent, and far too many choices offered, your child grabs hold of your authority and runs with it. And if expectations are nonnegotiable and you give your child a voice, he thinks he has a choice.

Colby loves to play the piano. He plays every chance he gets, becoming lost in his music creating songs and improvising with his assigned pieces. His music teacher says she sees more natural ability in Colby than she's ever seen in a child only ten years old, but he requires more discipline to practice and to push through the challenging pieces. Colby's mother, Liza, is thrilled with his talent. Though Colby clearly loves to play, his mother has a difficult time getting him to practice what's assigned by the music teacher. With the best of intentions, Liza wants to nurture her son's talent but she doesn't believe she has the power to influence it. She doesn't see the need to create fences related to how and when Colby will practice. The result: Colby doesn't practice.

Liza tried to convince Colby to practice. "Every day I ask him nicely to practice what his teacher assigned. I tell him how wonderfully he plays and how much I love listening to him. But I also tell him that in order to be great, he'll need to practice the material that's harder or maybe not as much fun."

Liza tried to bribe Colby to practice. "Last week, I promised to buy him new sheet music if he can get himself to the piano every afternoon and practice the pieces his music teacher assigned. But he just won't do it.

"It seems to have gotten worse after the recital he was supposed to play in last month. He was ready to play but he got a case of stage fright and he refused to go onstage. I begged him to go up there. I told him it was okay to be anxious but that he'd made a commitment; he had to play. Then the teacher tried to persuade him. The whole audience was aware of what was going on backstage. If he were four or five, maybe I could understand, but this was ridiculous. I sat there more embarrassed than I've been in a really long time. There's nothing I can do to make him practice or play if he doesn't want to."

The wavering parent provides no predictable structure, no regular routines aimed at preparing a child for accomplishing what is expected. She doesn't make it clear what part of the expectation is negotiable and which part is not. Liza talked. She begged and bribed, desperate to convince Colby to do what she wanted him to do. Colby's teacher pressed and pleaded; she believed she could talk Colby into playing, too. In situations where there is a lot of wavering, feelings rule. And expectations—though spoken—are never reinforced. Liza never prepared Colby for her expectations in advance and when in conflict over practicing or performing, she continued to negotiate. Because Liza is all talk and no action, Colby is never made to face the music.

Wondering Why You Waver?

Have you ever found yourself thinking you won't subject your child to what you were subjected to as a child? You won't yell. You won't spank. Your child won't be forced to behave in rigid, inflexible ways. You may be wavering because you're trying as hard as you can to reject the reactive parenting you experienced as a child.

Elaine acknowledges she wavers in creating fences for her two daughters. Yet she's beginning to realize her strong desire to set aside how she was parented has her parenting in a different yet equally ineffective manner.

"I try so hard not to appear demanding and controlling. My father didn't let me do or say anything he didn't approve of; I felt like I couldn't breathe without his permission. I want my girls to be able to think for themselves. But sometimes I feel like they take too many chances and aren't learning from their mistakes. I'm not sure giving them as much freedom as I do is working as well as I thought it would."

In Elaine's attempt to reject the reactive parenting style she experienced growing up, she's choosing to go to the other extreme. Elaine's so interested in rejecting her father's style, she's choosing to parent in the exact opposite way. Her father had many fences; she will have few. Her father offered little freedom; she will offer a lot. The parenting pendulum for Elaine and her children has swung from reactive parenting to wavering parenting. When you have not been exposed to proactive ways of parenting, there's a high likelihood you'll either adopt the style your parents had, or you'll try with all your might to reject it. It's not easy to find the middle ground when you're rejecting the style you were raised with.

Cathy describes herself as a free spirit. She's a painter and sees the world full of possibilities, not limitations. The mother of three young children with a fourth on the way, Cathy's beginning to realize her temperament and her role as mother may be out of sync.

"I'm an artist, and not one day looks like the next for me. I like it that way. But I know my children would behave better if things were more structured around here, if we had more routine. I think another reason I waver is because I don't know much about what children should be doing at certain ages. Should my two-year-old son be able to sit and listen to three stories at the library's story hour? Should I let my eighteen-month-old daughter give up her nap even though she's a bear by six o'clock? I'm having my fourth child, and I'm going to have to get some answers or I'm sunk."

Cathy wavers, like many parents, because she doesn't know what her fences should be. Unlike Elaine, Cathy isn't making a choice to outright resist creating them. She's just a person who doesn't need a lot of structure and routine to feel good, so she isn't compelled to create structure and routine for her children. Cathy also has a limited amount of information about child development and temperament, which makes it extra hard for her to create the right fences for her unique children.

Though this kind of information is vast and available, practical strategies specific to your child might elude you. Are you parenting without the day-to-day guidance of your parents, uncles, or sisters? Cathy's sister might have been able to tell her how to bridge the gap on her daughter's naptime or give her tips on how to help her son enjoy library story hour; if only she didn't live half a continent away. Geography is just one of the factors that can interfere with your support system.

Adding to the complexity of Cathy's situation, it's becoming increasingly clear that two of her three children need lots of structure, thrive best with predictable routines, and don't handle the unexpected very easily. Though Cathy may not need fences, her children surely will in order to behave their best.

Whether you waver because of the kind of parenting that was role modeled to you or simply because you don't know which fences are best, you can learn to balance nonnegotiable limits with age-appropriate freedom. We'll start by examining what you're teaching your child when you waver.

Draw the Line

Wavering parents, unlike proactive parents, seldom create ground rules for behaving in acceptable ways, and rarely—if ever—in advance of new or difficult situations. Life for the child of a wavering parent is unpredictable, with a great deal of focus on the freedom within the backyard, and an inadequate amount of attention paid to the fence itself.

> *Life for the child of a wavering parent is unpredictable, with a great deal of focus on the freedom within the backyard and an inadequate amount of attention paid to the fence itself.*

Described as accommodating and lenient, if you're a wavering parent you often don't see the need for fences until a troublesome situation arises and then are quick to find excuses for your child's misbehavior.

Expectations for behavior are centered mostly on what your

child *can do*, with most behavior falling in the negotiable category. If you waver, it's likely your expectations for behavior vacillate between expectations developmentally too high or too low. You may assume your child can make good decisions without your guidance and support, when he really doesn't have the ability or experience to do so. Or you may have expectations for his behavior set too low, allowing your child to get away with pushing limits when, given his age, he is more than able to accept limits and boundaries.

Your child comes to expect freedom without accountability, negotiating behavior big and small. Little attention is paid to what age-appropriate and respectful fences should look like because the focus is too heavily weighted on the freedom in the backyard. Your child is often presented with a garden fence when a stockade fence is required.

Family life is unstructured and supervision frequently too indirect and at times absent. Play time, bath time, and bedtime all blend together with absent or unclear expectations. Since the wavering parent often struggles with understanding what the appropriate expectations are given a child's development and temperament, often there are no expectations at all.

The wavering parent steps in with authority only when he's at a complete loss to get his child to accept the random and infrequent fences put forward. Even then, the wavering parent tries to reinforce rules and expectations with far too much talking.

The wavering parent steps in with authority only when he's at a complete loss to get his child to accept the random and infrequent fences put forward. Even then, the wavering parent tries to reinforce rules and expectations with far too much talking. While the wavering parent doesn't believe in discipline as punishment, emotions still run high in the wavering family. The wavering parent, feeling powerless to manage behavior, becomes exhausted and frustrated.

Fences are accepted by your child only when you get to the point of exasperation, becoming reactive in your attempt to get your child to do as he's been told. This begins a pattern of repeated wavering only to become reactive later.

While the reactive parent lectures, the wavering parent nags; both types of parents talk too much during periods of conflict. With heavy emphasis on explaining and convincing, the wavering parent makes nonnegotiable rules a set-up for a different kind of power struggle than the one experienced by the reactive parent. Every child pushes fences to find them. Yet when your child can't find a fence, he continues to behave in ways that are increasingly unacceptable. His efforts, whether conscious or not, are aimed at finding any kind of fence you're willing to build. When you don't build fences meant to influence behavior, you get dragged about by your child while each of you is holding the opposite end of the rope.

Molly spends less time with her seven-year-old son, Declan, than she'd like because of her work. She never wants the time they spend together to be negative. While she admits grocery shopping is a weekly nightmare for her and for Declan, she doesn't see how her wavering contributes to the problem. Every Tuesday after work, Molly and Declan pull into the parking lot of the local store and the negotiations begin. Declan is drawn to one of the junior-size carts—clearly not invented by a harried mother. Molly and Declan begin shopping, each with their respective carts. Declan puts whatever strikes his fancy into his miniature cart: chocolate candy bars, frosted donuts, and salty chips. While Molly tries to concentrate on her shopping, she encourages Declan to make better choices.

"Declan, you've chosen some really yummy snacks. But you'll be able to take only one treat, okay? Please put the rest back."

Declan makes no move to do so. And on they go to aisle three.

"I don't like that cereal; I want this one," he says, reaching for a sugary cereal he knows Molly dislikes.

"Oh no, you don't want that one. It's really bad for your teeth and you don't want to eat something that sugary before school."

"I want it and I'm going to get it," Declan demands.

"If you put it back, I'll let you pick out the cookies for school snack."

Plain and simple, Declan says no.

"All right, just this once," says Molly. "But you'll see you're not going to feel well if you don't eat a healthy breakfast. Maybe you'd like to take that to school for snack time instead of the cookies?"

Aisle eight looks the same as aisle three, negotiations taking place with every turn of their carts. Then Declan bumps into an elderly lady with his cart only to have Molly make the apology, not Declan. Molly smiles and excuses his behavior saying, "He loves to drive these little carts but he's not quite figured out the rules of the road. Are you okay?"

Molly tries to buy acceptable behavior from Declan with the promise of more freedom. "If you behave like a good boy, I'll let you get one more treat."

Maybe Molly gives Declan too much leeway because when she was a child her own freedom was denied. Or maybe she hands Declan freedom like a present because she's not able to give him the gift of her presence. Yet in all her attempts to avoid conflict, she just sets herself up for much more of it.

An Invitation to Misbehave

Negotiate. Discuss. Bargain. Seal the deal. These words are all synonyms; they mean the same thing. Do you really want to bargain with your child, reaching a deal with him over acceptable ways to behave? If you're a wavering parent, you give your child a voice when it comes to the things he really can't do and about fences he really needs to accept. And if an expectation isn't negotiable and you give your child a voice, he thinks he has a choice.

When you talk about nonnegotiable fences, you keep issues alive when they should be off the negotiating table. If you're talking, your child will talk, believing he has the power to choose whether he'll do what is right, respectful, and in some cases what is safe. And if these negotiations continue, he's right: He does have the choice to choose.

The wavering parent nags, telling her child repeatedly to do something while being ignored. Since requests and directions are continually spoken and often from a distance they're rarely acted upon, the child doubts these expectations or limits will ever be enforced. And if it's all talk and no action, once again the child is right: He has the choice to choose.

Davis walks his three-year-old daughter, Lucy, into the restaurant where his five-year-old niece's birthday party is being held. Before he sends Lucy off to the table where her cousins are sitting he says, "You're going to be good, okay, Lucy?"

Lucy nods her head and runs to meet up with her cousins, nearly tripping a waitress carrying a large tray full of drinks. Davis sighs and takes a seat at a different table, where the adults have gathered.

Almost immediately, Lucy begins behaving in unacceptable ways. She stands on her chair. She blows bubbles into her soda. She takes the basket of rolls and says, "All of these are mine."

Davis looks on from his table and tosses directions from across the room like a boomerang. "Lucy, please behave. Lucy, can you sit down? Honey, you really need to share those rolls with all your cousins. I'll get you more if they run out, okay?"

Lucy chooses to dismiss Davis's limits because he is making them negotiable. She doesn't need to sit down or share the rolls. After Lucy stands up again and begins to throw rolls across the table at her cousin, Davis shouts, "Lucy, you need to stop that and sit down. How would you like it if someone threw a roll at you?"

But Lucy's out-of-bounds behavior continues because there aren't any fences. Davis is sending requests and commands to Lucy from a distance. Davis talks about the rules without matching a rule to an action. He thinks he's making certain behavior nonnegotiable but he's talking—repeatedly talking—and making his expectations for Lucy something she has the option of choosing or ignoring. Lucy ignores.

The wavering parent builds fences with wishy-washy language, frequently posing limits as questions. "Do you want to go to bed?" "How about some broccoli?" "Would you like to do your homework now?" Maybe you have a child who will say yes, in which case wonderful. No problem. But most of you will more likely hear your child say no. Perhaps you won't even get a verbal acknowledgment; your child will just continue doing what he's doing, not listening to you at all.

If you pose limits as questions, be prepared for all kinds of answers, including "No," and "Not now." You really can't become frustrated or angry at your child if she rejects your attempt at building a fence. After all, you asked her a question in which one of the possible answers is "No."

Do you feel like you state limits in a clear and direct manner and still your child discounts them? The wavering parent has been known to build a fence with a declarative statement only to follow it with the gate-opening word: *Okay.* "It's time for bed, okay? You must eat your broccoli, okay?" Once the word *okay* is added to the end of a limit, it makes that limit negotiable. And be careful of building fences with abstract language. You might think you're being clear and direct when you say to your child "Work it out," or "You need to cooperate." But those words don't have concrete meaning to your child. What does *work it out* or *cooperate* really mean? Be specific: Use phrases like *Take turns, Trade one toy for another,* or *It's your turn when the timer goes off.* Convey your precise meaning.

You've heard the expression "Actions speak louder than words." In studies looking at effective communication, three elements emerge as the most important factors: the words you speak, your tone of voice, and your body language, gestures, and actions. Believe it or not, less than 10 percent of what you communicate is related to the words you speak. And when your words are wishy-washy and vague, it's no wonder your child doesn't take your verbal direction. This is where action becomes powerful. If Davis wants Lucy to sit down at her table, he can gently sit her down. If Davis wants Lucy to stop blowing bubbles with her straw, he can move her drink. If Davis wants to keep rolls from hurling through the air, he can take the basket. Davis's actions can and will speak louder, more respectfully and effectively to Lucy—inviting her to behave.

Freedom Isn't Free

When the messages you give your child are all talk and no action, your child starts a desperate search for fences. Every child—in fact, every person—needs boundaries for physical and emotional safety. If you're a wavering parent, your child's freedom is abundant, so his behavior will predictably escalate in an attempt to force you to show him where the boundaries for behavior are hidden. Though this might look to you like a demand for more freedom, it's really an effort on your child's part to find the fence and figure out the size of his backyard.

The child of a wavering parent learns his boundaries are something he must hunt for, as they're not readily provided. Unfortunately, the older your child gets the more regularly he's received the message he doesn't need to do what you tell him to do. If he doesn't have to do what you tell him to do, why would he need to listen to anyone else?

Bernie, a six-year-old boy is having a difficult time accepting the fences for behavior at school. His first-grade teacher, Mr. Matthews, has called a conference with Bernie's mother. He begins by sharing what a bright and interesting boy Bernie is, then moves on to share how concerned he is that Bernie looks for every opportunity to test the fences at school.

Bernie runs in the hallway. He leaves the classroom at will. He takes other students' snacks if he likes them better than his own. The list goes on and on. Bernie's mother tearfully says she's not surprised. She's always found it hard to parent Bernie; his behavior looks much the same at home.

While Mr. Matthews is working hard to hold Bernie accountable for behavior in class, Bernie's behavior is out of control in the cafeteria and on the bus. He throws food in the cafeteria and dumps his trash on the floor. He teases children on the bus, forcing others to give him their seats. According to the cafeteria monitors and the bus driver, they've tried to tell Bernie what they expect of him. But he's said to them on a number of occasions, "I don't have to listen to you because I don't have to listen to anyone."

It's a telling remark. If Bernie isn't expected to accept fences at home from his parent—the ultimate authority in the life of any child—why would he see the need to accept fences from the cafeteria workers and bus driver? Bernie has little practice accepting fences. In his experience, rules are meant to be broken. Rules apply to others, not him.

The wavering parent lacks decisiveness. If your child is looking for direction, guidance, and clear authority from you and you won't make a decision, he'll take the decision-making power into his own hands and decide for both of you. The child with limitless power, too much decision-making authority, and no fences finds safety and security only when behavior gets so out of control someone finally intervenes to contain him. The child, who must get out of control to find his fences, will be labeled a troublemaker, entitled, spoiled, a brat. Like Bernie, any child of a wavering parent will pay a heavy price for having too much freedom. He won't be able to find and respect the boundaries created to help him behave in socially acceptable ways; and he'll be disliked because of it.

> *If your child is looking for direction, guidance, and clear authority from you and you won't make a decision, he'll take the decision-making power into his own hands and decide for both of you.*

Taking risks looking for fences

When a child is raised with too much freedom or a backyard too big for her age, daily life is a series of negotiations. Wheeling and dealing, your child learns nothing is off limits to her, *no* is a meaningless word, and desires are rewarded with more power and control. The negotiations begin with talking and begging but when those techniques don't get the child what she wants, she'll resort to more mischievous behavior aimed at getting her way or getting your attention.

Whining, screaming, and demanding behavior is used to continue the negotiations, leading others to view your child as difficult and unlikable. Yet no child behaves in these ways because she wants to be disliked. The child of a parent who wavers is simply behaving in challenging ways in response to never feeling or seeing age-appropriate fences. I assure you, she wants them.

When presented with the occasional fence from her parent or with fences from other authority figures, she has no experience accepting them. While no parent wants his child to be disliked or judged for behaving in entitled and uncooperative ways, the child who cannot accept fences is judged. Over time, the fence-seeking child of a wavering parent will be judged so often she'll begin to feel disliked, left out, and unloved. Once she sees herself as not liked and not accepted, she may as well treat herself with the same disrespect she feels from those around her.

> *The child with solid fences, good communication with her parents, and consistent, predictable boundaries for behavior feels good about herself; she feels loved. Every child—even your teenager—wants guidance, protection, affection, and yes—supervision. Your child wants nonnegotiable, immovable boundaries, provided by you.*

Fifteen-year-old Patrice may seem like a typical teenager. She goes to school, likes to spend time on the computer, and she loves to hang out with her friends. But Patrice is experimenting with some of the most dangerous temptations adolescents play with today. She drinks alcohol most weekends, doing whatever she can to fit in with a popular group of girls from school. She cuts herself on occasion, wanting to do something extreme, to feel something intense. She searches online chat rooms for other teens who feel like she does: confused, unpopular, and alone.

Unsupervised teenagers are looking for fences in the bottom of a bottle, in online chat rooms, and in the arms of other teens at alarmingly high rates. Believe me when I say teenagers like Patrice are tempted by and take part in risky behavior because they can. The teen with a secret life is unsupervised, lacking fences; she acts out in dramatic ways to draw attention to her need for security, restraint, and love. But not all teenagers have a secret life.

The child with solid fences, good communication with her parents, and consistent, predictable boundaries for behavior feels good about herself; she feels loved. Every child—even your teenager—wants guidance, protection, affection, and yes—supervision. Your child wants nonnegotiable, immovable boundaries, provided by you.

Drop the Rope

No one can force you to negotiate if you don't want to negotiate. What would happen to the wavering dynamic in your family if you suddenly stopped negotiating away your power? If you've ever been water-skiing you know when you let go of your end of the rope, the boat is no longer able to drag you through the water. When you drop the rope between you and your child, he won't be able to drag you about either. Your child's struggle for power and control will end because you won't be giving away your authority. When negotiations over nonnegotiable boundaries end, only then are you presented with a real opportunity to parent more effectively.

To learn how to drop the rope, first you'll need to recognize when you're negotiating over that which is not negotiable. Figure out your fences in advance. Talk with your child's other parent about fences you can agree on for mealtime, bedtime, and playtime; all the routines of daily living that require clear boundaries. Once you have established your nonnegotiable rules, communicate them to your child in a calm moment; then be prepared to step in with action if or when fences are breeched. Your goal is to teach your child when he bumps up against a nonnegotiable limit—the talking is over.

When you talk, choose positive language without qualifiers like the word *okay*. Go to your child and provide simple, direct limits. Directions given from a distance invite fence pushing. And most important, stop talking when you realize you're in conflict. Remember, the actions you take, especially in conflict, are enormously powerful in teaching your child about fences. At first, finding the appropriate actions might seem challenging, but simple actions are always there and they're always smaller than you think.

When you choose direct ways of creating fences, following through, and delivering messages about behavior, you'll be on your way to teaching your child to behave well. Your child will learn to accept fences while still enjoying the freedom within the backyard. She'll learn how to respond to physical and emotional boundaries and still make good choices, at every age.

In the next chapter, I'll share with you all you'll need to know to parent more proactively. When you adopt a more proactive style, you'll enjoy more family harmony, your child will behave better, and the two of you will enjoy a deeper, richer relationship. You'll want to spend time with her because you truly like her and have fun with her—and other people will feel the same way. Remember, if it's not negotiable, why are you still talking?

7. Learning to Be Proactive

Firefighter Reed prepares one of the classrooms of the newly renovated elementary school for tonight's lecture on fire safety. He places the new fire extinguishers on the front table as parents and teachers enter and take their seats.

He's well into the lecture when a concerned parent raises his hand and says, "I don't mean to interrupt but there's only fifteen minutes left and all we've talked about is what to do if there's a fire. We haven't heard anything about how we're going to prevent one. I'm just as interested, if not more so, in teaching the children fire prevention."

Suddenly there's a buzz spreading throughout the room. Parents and teachers start brainstorming effective ways to teach the children about fire prevention. One parent suggests giving the children a tour of the building before school starts in September, appointing older children as fire marshals, and giving every child a coloring book to review fire safety tips for home and for school.

Another parent proposes giving the children advance notice of fire drills since many of the younger children are frightened the first time they hear a fire alarm.

These parents begin to anticipate what the children need to learn and then create a plan for teaching this critical information. By the end of the training, the focus has shifted dramatically away from fire extinguishers and on to prevention. Their fire safety plan becomes more focused on how to prevent a fire than how to put one out. With a variety of strategies aimed at teaching the children the safety rules and expectations in advance, these parents and teachers are more prepared than ever to prevent an unacceptable situation from happening in the first place.

When you're interested in undoing a behavior that has already happened, quite often repeatedly, behaviorists like me call it trying to extinguish behavior. By the time you're looking for a behavior extinguisher, you've already got smoke. And where there's smoke there's fire.

When I conduct parenting workshops, the number one question I get is, "What do I do when he _____?" Fill in the blank with anything from "won't do his homework" to "calls her brother a name" to "wears his muddy shoes all through the house." The problem with asking questions that begin with "what do I do when . . ." is that you're assuming the behavior has already occurred. You're waiting until you're in conflict. When you're interested in undoing a behavior that has already happened, quite often repeatedly, behaviorists like me call it trying to extinguish behavior. By the time you're looking for a behavior extinguisher, you've already got smoke. And where there's smoke there's fire.

There are effective ways to extinguish behavior, which I promise to share with you, but don't you agree it would be better to prevent misbehavior from happening in the first place? In behavior management, like fire safety, prevention is best. Prevention is powerful. Prevention is proactive.

Proactive Discipline

Your son won't do his homework. You daughter calls her brother a name. Your five-year-old wears his muddy shoes all through the house. If any of these behaviors has occurred only once, you're not likely to be bothered by it. Yet if these or any other behavior makes you feel angry or powerless, the behavior has happened repeatedly. Actions that occur repeatedly constitute patterns of behavior. And remember, if something happens once, it's once. If it happens again, it's a theme. The themes in your child's behavior require a prevention plan, not just a plan to deal with or extinguish misbehavior.

Leigh looks out her front window and sees three of her son's friends coming up the street. Eight-year-old Drew and his friends love riding scooters and bikes around the neighborhood. Before the boys make it to the front door, Leigh says to Drew, "Your friends are going to be here any minute. If you're going to ride scooters this morning, can you tell me what you'll need to remember?"

Without stopping to think Drew replies, "Knee pads and a helmet. I forgot yesterday but I'll wear them today, I promise. Can I go now?"

"Yes. But before you do, I want you to know I expect you to wear your safety gear. Should you forget, like yesterday, I'll come outside to remind you. Now go have fun and be safe."

By being proactive, Leigh just increased the chances Drew will accept her fence for scooter riding. When you increase your proactive discipline, you decrease conflict—or the need to extinguish behavior. Leigh could have been reactive, waiting until she looked out the window to see Drew riding his scooter for the second day in a row without pads and a helmet. Angry to see the same behavior again after she'd given him a good talking-to, she might storm outside yelling and threatening, finally taking the scooter away.

Her goal: to drive her point home, getting him to see she means business.

Or Leigh could have wavered. She may have told Drew how important the rule was but upon seeing him without the gear, do nothing to reinforce her expectation. Maybe she would nag him several times from the doorway to go get the gear. Maybe she'd talk to him more about the rule, the next time he came in for a glass of water. Though told repeatedly to use the gear, Drew would still have been riding without it. Perhaps he'd see a fence, but one with the gate wide open.

Leigh chose to be proactive. She anticipated the likelihood her eight-year-old son would be so eager to play with his friends he'd act impulsively, not defiantly. He'd needed reminding before—just yesterday in fact—so today she'd need to be clear about her fence for riding scooters. Leigh told him once more how she'd reinforce the fence if he didn't accept it. She chose to get her point across with positive language and actions that made sense to this situation. She didn't use dramatic language and gestures or take away the scooter, because this would do nothing to teach Drew to remember his gear. Instead, she respected Drew enough to show him the fence again.

What do you think Drew did when he walked from the house to his scooter? Did he put on his pads and helmet before joining his friends for a ride? If you believe like I do, that when presented with clear fences your child will accept them, then you think Drew followed Leigh's rule.

If you believe a child will push every fence he's presented with, you might think he refused to accept Leigh's rule. I disagree with the popular thinking that every child misbehaves first and accepts fences later. Either way you look at it, Leigh is prepared.

If he follows the rule, they both win. He does as he's been told. If he doesn't follow the rule and she goes outside to hand him the pads and helmet without talking, they both still win: Leigh because she told him what she expected, and then showed him she meant what she said; Drew because his mother built a good solid fence, and when he pushed open the gate, she closed it.

Tell-me, Show-me Learning

Skills, attitudes, and values are taught. Learning takes place whenever a new connection is made between one thing and another where prior to the teaching no such connection existed.

At a very young age, your child learns by making these connections between a thought, feeling, or action and another thought, feeling, or action. If you feed your baby every time he cries, he comes to expect to be fed each time he cries. If your one-year-old drops a toy from her high chair and you laugh while you pick it up, watch for her to do it again and again. This is called cause-and-effect learning. The way you parent should encourage your child to learn in cause-and-effect ways, so he or she will form healthy connections between thoughts, feelings, and actions.

The proactive parent recognizes she can take advantage of her child's ability to learn in cause-and-effect ways. She teaches a healthy connection when she connects what she tells her child with what her child experiences. Like the proactive parent, your power lies in teaching your child you mean what you say, not in trying to undo negative behavior.

When you build a fence, I call it *tell-me discipline:* You can talk, converse, and discuss. This is the time your child finds out what is negotiable and what is not. When you're in conflict and you follow through by doing what you told your child you would do, I call it *show-me discipline*—and now the talking is over.

Natalia tells her son about her new fence for dinner. She will only call him once; after she does, dinner will begin with or without him. The next evening, she calls him once and then sits down for dinner. A few minutes later he hears laughter and talking and comes to join the meal. He asks, "Why are you eating without me?"

Natalia responds with, "I call only once for dinner. Here, fill your plate and tell us about your day."

Tell-me discipline, show-me discipline. Cause-and-effect learning. Your child learns best when what you say equals what you do. If you say you don't allow ball playing in the house, then your child mustn't play ball in the house. In *tell-me discipline*, you review the rules with your child whenever you like, as long as he's not playing ball in the house. In *show-me discipline*, you intervene each and every time he plays ball in the house.

Let's say you've done a nice job with your tell-me discipline and you've made it clear to your son that there's no ball in the house. Later that day or week, you see him playing ball in the house. Is there really anything else you have to *say?* Or should you simply put your hand out to accept the ball or direct your son to the yard? Tell-me, show-me discipline helps both you and your child differentiate between what's negotiable and what's not. It's a lot easier to use show-me discipline, if you've initiated the tell-me discipline outside of conflict. The key is to anticipate where fences need to be built.

Predict and Prevent

Melissa puts the finishing touches on a dozen beautifully frosted cupcakes for the school bake sale. Placing them on the kitchen table, she dashes to the front hall to get her coat and bag. As Melissa heads in one direction, her four-year-old twins come into the kitchen from the den, spy the cupcakes, and . . .

Human behavior is predictable. What do you suppose Melissa's four-year-old twins do? What would you do if faced with a sugary confection frosted to perfection? Will they take a bite or just a swipe of frosting? Perhaps they won't touch them at all. You guessed correctly if you figured one twin took a luscious cupcake and savored his every bite, while the other twin dared only take a careful swipe, leaving his chosen cupcake seemingly untouched.

You can predict with some degree of certainty what your child will do in any given situation and because you can, you can take action to avoid conflict.

Melissa knows her children; she could have predicted their response to this temptation. And because she could have predicted it, she could have prevented it.

No one knows your child better than you do. You know what your child is likely to do if faced with those tasty treats. Yet most parents don't use this valuable information to their advantage as often as they could or should. You can predict with some degree of certainty what your child will do in any given situation. And because you can, an important part of teaching your child to behave well is to avoid putting him in situations where he'll behave poorly. You can take action to avoid conflict.

If you aren't sure whether your daughter will eat one, swipe one, or leave the cupcakes untouched, I recommend you make decisions about prevention based on what's most likely to happen along with what you're willing and able to teach. You don't think Melissa put the cupcakes there to test her children's ability to resist temptation, do you? She either thinks her twins are capable of recognizing the cupcakes are off limits or she just got busy and didn't take the time to set her children up for success.

Since she isn't focused on teaching her four-year-old twins to resist temptation and she doesn't have time to make more cupcakes, she shouldn't take her chances. Without predicting and preventing, conflict for Melissa is literally around the corner. If she predicts what will happen in this situation, she has more options. She might put her coat and bag over the kitchen chair before she frosts the cupcakes. She might place the cupcakes up high when she goes to get her coat. She might bring her twins with her as she collects her belongings. Melissa has the choice to stay out of conflict but to do so she needs to be proactive. She needs to anticipate what her children will do and plan accordingly. She knows what her children will do here and elsewhere—and so do you.

Predict and Prepare

More often than not, conflict is avoidable. Yet sometimes conflict happens. There are those times when you aren't able to predict and then prevent. Or maybe you can predict but choose not to prevent. Maybe you'd rather teach your child to see cupcakes and resist the urge to eat one. If so, then instead of predicting and preventing, you can predict behavior and prepare your child to accept your fence. But it's very important that you know you have a choice.

You can predict and prevent or you can predict and prepare. But if you wait until your child eats a cupcake and then you ask *what do I do when he does that*, you're in conflict trying to find a strategy aimed at extinguishing behavior—behavior you knew was quite possible and highly probable.

The power to shape behavior doesn't lie in wavering—"I guess I don't really mind that he ate the cupcakes for the bake sale." Or in reacting—"I can't believe you ate those cupcakes, you knew they were for the bake sale; go to time-out." Your power to shape behavior lies in being proactive. You get to choose whether you'll prevent predictable behavior or prepare your child to behave in ways you consider more acceptable.

Seven-year-old Eleanor has such a painful sore throat she's missed school for the second day in a row. Her dad, Dan, has scheduled a visit to the pediatrician for later this morning. Dan knows his daughter finds going to the doctor difficult even when it's just a well visit. He anticipates she'll have difficulty with this visit, especially since she'll need a swab test for strep throat.

"Eleanor, your sore throat might go away on its own or you might need medicine to feel better. Only Dr. Lewis can tell for sure. You and I are going to go see Dr. Lewis at 11:00 this morning."

"I don't want to go to the doctor's. I feel better, Daddy, really I do."

Dan predicted Eleanor wasn't going to like the idea of a visit to the doctor. Dan's decided a visit to the doctor is a nonnegotiable fence. He's not able to prevent this potential source of conflict for Eleanor. But he doesn't need to wait until he and Eleanor experience conflict to teach her this fence isn't negotiable; Dan prepares Eleanor to accept the nonnegotiable aspects of her doctor's appointment.

"I know you don't want to go but you must. I'll come in with you. You can hold my hand or you can sit on my lap. Dr. Lewis or one of the nurses will do the test on your throat. I know you hate the feeling when they put the stick to the back of your throat but when you cooperate it goes a lot faster. It's okay for you not to like it but we won't leave the office until it's done. And when we get there, I won't be discussing this again. Do you have any questions?"

Dan's prepared Eleanor for what she can expect. He's told her what is negotiable and what is not. She has a chance to ask questions and she does.

"Am I going to get a shot, too?"

"I don't think so. But I'm not sure. Either you or I can ask Dr. Lewis when we get there. You might need medicine, though. I know you don't like pills so I'll ask for a liquid. Would you like to get some Popsicles on the way home or would you rather have freeze pops?"

Dan talks about what Eleanor can do. But do you notice how he doesn't continue to discuss what Eleanor *can't* do? Once the fence is made clear, he stops talking about it. When they arrive at the doctor's office, he reminds Eleanor what she can do, keeping the focus on her freedom to sit holding his hand or to sit on his lap. She may ask Dr. Lewis a question or not, but she gets the throat culture. It's irrelevant whether she's happy about it or not; getting the culture isn't negotiable.

> *When you increase preparation, you decrease conflict. When you give your child the benefit of knowing what she can expect, only then is she able to focus on what she has control over.*

When you increase preparation, you decrease conflict. When you give your child the benefit of knowing what she can expect, only then is she able to focus on what she has control over. She feels the safety and security of the fence, accepting what's not negotiable along with what is. Eleanor, at age seven, was not given the power to choose whether or not to get a throat culture but she was given age-appropriate freedoms like choosing between popsicles or freeze pops.

Practice Makes (Almost) Perfect

Playing the clarinet. Shooting free throws in basketball. Walking on a balance beam. Flying a kite. Practice often and you'll get better playing, shooting, walking, and flying. Your child may be a natural athlete or musician; the skills are solid but most find that success in reading music or playing a game rests on how much you practice.

Vicarious learning is a fancy name for the learning that comes from practicing new skills to be learned or from watching the experiences of others. With opportunities to practice everything from how to walk in the house to how to answer the phone, your child can learn very effectively, especially if practice is repetitive.

There are two kinds of vicarious learning you can use to guide your child. The first involves training. Five-year-olds copy letters from books. Ten-year-olds imitate the characteristic stance of famous baseball players. Your daughter rehearses her play. Your son practices lining up for graduation. In the rehearsing and practicing, your child is learning. He's learning from what's modeled. He's getting a taste of how real situations may look and feel. She's learning what she can and can't do to be successful. She gets a shot at situations before she's expected to perform for real.

Vicarious or simulated learning gets your child as close to the real thing as possible. This kind of learning counts—a lot. Without the stress found in real life circumstances, your child has the opportunity to build skill.

Playing restaurant at home helps the reluctant child order his milk in the real restaurant later. Rehearsing what she'll say on a job interview helps your tentative teenager prepare for her actual job interview.

The second kind of vicarious learning involves learning from the missteps of others. When your child's best friend doesn't study for a test and gets a D, or his cousin loses his job for failing to show up time and time again, your child is learning. Your child can learn about fences by looking at other people's backyards. It might be tempting to use only positive experiences to teach positive behavior, but vicarious learning about the negative experiences of others is equally valuable. You certainly don't want or need your child to experience everything firsthand in order to learn about your fences and the freedoms to be found in your backyard.

Use both the positive and negative experiences of others to

teach. Talk to your daughter about what happened to her friend when she asked for extra help from the teacher and aced the test. Talk to your son about the classmate who drank while driving and got in a fender-bender. Your daughter can learn about your fences for schoolwork without having to fail first. And your son can learn what your fences are for social behavior without drinking too much and getting in an accident.

Opportunities for vicarious learning are all around you; use them wisely. Vicarious learning works best when positive behavior is modeled and practiced and when you and your child talk outside of conflict. Conversing—not lecturing or nagging—communicates expectations. Assume your child wants to learn to behave well; he just needs someone to show him how.

ACT—Act Consistently with Timeliness

Okay, so you didn't predict. You forgot to prevent. And you didn't encourage your child to practice. Now what? Every parent finds herself in conflict from time to time without having predicted, prevented, prepared or practiced. And still you have options for helping your child accept fences. When your child bumps up against a nonnegotiable limit, even if she hasn't been forewarned—the talking is over. You can ACT: act consistently with timeliness.

In conflict, actions speak louder than words. When your child pushes fences, you can extinguish behavior in two powerful yet simple ways: with small actions and nonverbal cues. Neither involves talking so your child is less likely to think your expectations are negotiable. Because if it's not negotiable, then of course you won't be talking.

Using small actions to communicate is far simpler than the more dramatic time-out, taking away privileges, or grounding. In contrast to those popular parenting techniques, small actions teach how to do something differently in the future because the action fits the behavior. When you find yourself in a situation you didn't predict or prevent or prepare for, use appropriate actions to deliver your message. If your son needs to use soap when he washes his hands, hand him the soap. When your daughter needs to put her shoes on, hand her the shoes.

When you talk, plead, and nag, you make ordinary events into potential power struggles between you and your child, with each of you focused on figuring out who's in charge. But when you use small actions, meaning is conveyed very clearly and the option to resist is reduced, if not eliminated.

Kat and her two-year-old, Taylor, stop off at a convenience store to grab a gallon of milk and the newspaper. Kat assumes it's a quick in-and-out errand so she doesn't prepare Taylor in any way. Once inside the store, Kat sees she'll need to wait in line to purchase her items. Taylor sees all the snacks lined up at eye level and is tempted to touch. Without talking, Kat puts back the first snack Taylor takes from the rack. She then takes hold of his hand. Taylor's next attempt at lifting snacks comes when he escapes from her grasp and goes to grab another treat. Kat, without talking, puts the milk and paper on the counter and picks Taylor up. Throughout this fence building and fence pushing, Kat is talking to Taylor. But not about candy and gum. "Look Taylor, see the truck outside. It's a fire truck. Would you like to play trucks when we get home?"

Milk and paper in one hand and Taylor in her arms, Kat successfully manages to deliver a clear message. Without saying there will be no candy today and without giving in to the pressure to buy a snack to keep Taylor behaving well, Kat communicates a clear message to Taylor, one he must accept because it's not negotiable.

You might think you're taking action when you send your child to his room or you take away a trip to the movies. But those actions are big overreactions to behavior you object to. The reactive parent tends to use big actions instead of small ones and often adds negative language to any action taken. The wavering parent tends to take little to no action, assuming tell-me discipline will be enough to change behavior.

The proactive parent uses small actions such as gently sitting a child down in his high chair to indicate no standing up. Or moving the milk from the table to the counter to say no more milk. Or handing a child paper towels to say clean up what you've spilled on the floor. Small actions are exactly that: tiny steps you take to deliver your message.

Another powerful way to communicate without making situations negotiable is through the use of nonverbal cues. Putting one finger to your lips says *shhhh*. Putting your hand out says hand me the car keys. There are millions of gestures that communicate meaning, and once again this aspect of using action to convey expectation is underutilized. Your child knows what you mean when you tap his homework paper instead of repeatedly saying, do your homework. Patting the chair says sit here. Pointing to a backpack or other object says pick it up. When you find yourself in conflict, do you think the only way to share expectations is by using more tell-me discipline? The truth is, conflict calls for less tell-me discipline and more show-me discipline. Nonverbal cueing diffuses powerful emotions and doesn't distract your child from the job at hand. And nonverbal gestures don't fuel intensity or encourage power struggles.

Joshua loves television so much he's often mesmerized by it, dis-

> *Another powerful way to communicate without making situations negotiable is through non-verbal cues. Putting one finger to your lips says shhhh. Putting your hand out says hand me the car keys. There are millions of gestures that communicate meaning.*

regarding everything else going on around him. Tonight, Joshua's mother, Paige, has been focused on making a nice family dinner; letting the time slip away from her, allowing Joshua to watch more television. Finally the meal is ready and she calls all of her children to the table. Everyone comes except Joshua. She calls him again. And before the words are fully out of her mouth, Paige realizes she's in conflict. She heads to the den. She starts with a nonverbal cue to get Joshua's attention; she knocks on the door.

In a semifocused fashion, Joshua asks, "What?"

"Dinner," Paige says. Simple, direct, and not negotiable. But Joshua's previous experience tells him, just keep watching television. She's called him so many times before, why would this time be any different?

"I'll be there in ten minutes. I'm going to watch the rest of my show," Joshua says distractedly.

Calmly, Paige walks in front of the television and points to the power button. "You or me," she says.

Joshua says, "Hey, get out of the way."

Paige reaches over to the television and shuts it off.

"I was watching that."

"Are you having a salad or green beans for your vegetable tonight?"

Paige used nonverbal cueing and small action to convey her expectation. Are you skeptical of the power of small action and nonverbal cueing? Do you doubt your child would come as willingly as Joshua did? It's possible your child has more difficulty accepting fences, but it's also possible you've responded to your child in a similar situation by repeatedly talking about whether he should watch television or eat with the family while dinner gets colder and colder. You've got to try small action and nonverbal cueing to believe in it; it's show-me discipline. And show-me discipline works best in conflict.

Certainly your power to shape behavior lies in being proactive. It's always best to have predicted an upcoming challenge and then either prevent resistant behavior or prepare your child for what you expect. There is a time to talk.

After that, it's time to stop talking. It's time to act. Once in conflict, more talking simply shines a spotlight on behavior you find unacceptable. Small actions and nonverbal cues extinguish behavior and deliver clearer messages about the behavior that isn't up for discussion.

A Time to Talk

When your child's behavior is thematic and predictable, creating a proactive plan for teaching good behavior is necessary. You'll want to use a combination of tell-me and show-me discipline to build your fences and show your child exactly what he can and can't do.

All behavior tells a story. And if the same behavior happens repeatedly, you have a theme. Thematic behavior is often connected to your child's temperament. Regardless of why your child is behaving in a particular manner, your child needs new and better ways to behave more successfully.

In Part III, the section on your child's style, I'll explore in detail how to deal with temperament since your child's predictable style of behaving has a lot to do with how she accepts fences. Keep in mind, in thematic behavioral situations, you'll need much more than small actions and nonverbal cueing to help your child learn how to manage situations he always finds difficult. You'll need a proactive plan that clearly communicates specifically what your child can and can't do.

Four-year-old Nathan loves playing in his sandbox, until his little sister, May, decides to play there. Over the last couple of days,

Lena, their mother, has seen the situation go from bad to worse. Nathan, who'd rather play alone, throws sand and grabs toys. Lena believes both children can learn to play well in the sandbox but Nathan is going to need more help.

Today, before going outside, she talks with Nathan about what she expects. She tells him he'll have some time to play alone with the toys in the sandbox. Then there will be some time he'll play with his sister in the sandbox. If May takes one of his toys, he can ask for his mother's help or trade toys with May. But he can not throw sand at his sister. They practice trading and talk about which words Nathan can use to get his mother's help should he need it. Lena gives Nathan what I call *can-dos* for this situation—all the things he can do to work things out and play well. She'll also remind him with action, though only if she must, that throwing sand is unacceptable.

A Time to Act

It's time to use small actions when the behavior you object to is safety related and when the small actions are obvious to you. If your child gets out of bed at night, walk him back. If your child throws a toy, take the toy. If he speaks disrespectfully to you, walk away from him. Small actions should be used when it makes sense to you and your child. Small actions are always available to you. They're right there in the situation and they're always smaller than you think.

Do you think Lena's proactive plan was successful? Could Lena have set Nathan up for success so he'll never again have difficulty sharing his sand toys with his sister? It's doubtful, if she only expects to use tell-me discipline. It's also doubtful if she only expects to use show-me discipline once. But it's absolutely possible if Lena prepares Nathan and then steps in with show-me discipline each and every time he pushes this fence. Her job is to make it clear to Nathan how he's expected to play, using tell-me and show-me discipline.

Lena takes the children outside to play. Shortly after they enter the sandbox, Lena uses a gesture to remind Nathan he can trade the toy May just took from him with another toy. She uses the small actions of giving the toy back to May after Nathan grabs it, moving the children to separate sides of the sandbox, and finally walks Nathan to the swing set. It isn't long before Nathan comes to understand if he wants to play, he'll have to follow the rules for playing in the sandbox with his sister. He pleads to be given another chance to play well. Lena says he's welcome to play if he follows the rules. She believes if he's going to learn how to play well, he should be given the chance to try again. But if he continues to have difficulty, she'll stop the play and give him another chance another day.

A Time to Parent

When you're proactive you may rarely need to extinguish unacceptable behavior. But if you're only willing to extinguish behavior, you're going to have a much more difficult time influencing behavior in a positive way. Are you thinking that being a proactive parent sounds like it's going to take a lot of time? All parenting takes time, no matter how you choose to do it.

If you're a reactive parent, parenting takes time. Time is spent reacting—sometimes overreacting—to predictable and thematic behavior. There's that rope between you and your child, and you spend precious time pulling and tugging against your child's desire for power and control. You go from fire to fire trying to extinguish misbehavior every chance you get.

If you're a wavering parent, parenting takes time. You spend time trying to determine whether behavior is acceptable or not. Your indecision is a decision to let your child drag you about by the rope as you struggle for power and authority. Yet your child has the power to continue behaving any way he pleases regardless of what others want him to do. Time is spent negotiating the nonnegotiable, which gives your child the message he's in charge, not you.

Yes, being a proactive parent takes time. But it is time well spent, for the child of a proactive parent sees and respects fences. She chooses to behave because it's the right thing to do, not out of fear of punishment. Skills for handling change and stress and the word *no* are taught and accepted. Any way you look at it, parenting takes time. The question is: How do you want to spend your time?

part three
Their Style

8. Children Who Push Fences

Maggie loves to read bedtime stories each night to her three-year-old son. Julian, already in his footy pajamas, snuggles under the covers and eagerly awaits tonight's story. "*The Tale of Peter Rabbit* by Beatrix Potter," Maggie begins. The story opens with four little bunnies going off for a day of play in the fields and on the lane. The bunnies' mother warns them of the dangers they may face if they disregard her rules. Julian is paying close attention to this, his favorite of the *Peter Rabbit* series.

Three of the four bunnies follow their mother's directions; Peter Rabbit does not. He not only finds his safety in jeopardy but he loses his coat, and later loses his supper.

When Maggie finishes reading, Julian says, "Mommy, Peter's like me. I forget the rules sometimes, too."

"Everyone forgets once in a while, Julian. It's the mommy's job to help her bunny remember."

In the beginning of my workshops, I ask, "How many of you

have more than one child?" Inevitably, almost all the audience members raise their hands. Then I ask, "How many of you have children who are exactly alike?" The results of my informal poll are always the same—not one person raises his or her hand. If you have more than one bunny, you know they're not alike, so why would the fences you create for them be the same? You might have one or two children who accept fences easily and adapt to changing expectations without difficulty, and you might have one child for whom accepting fences and adapting to changing expectations is hard on him, on you, and on your whole family.

As illustrated by countless children's stories, there are some children who push fences more than others do. The child who pushes fences more, does so to find the physical and emotional boundaries he needs to feel good and do well. You may not care if your child experiences the natural results of his behavior, but you shouldn't want all your child's learning to come through negative experiences.

A Different Kind of Blame Game

Although there's a tendency to blame parents for a child's unacceptable behavior, the child also gets blamed. She's a brat. He's spoiled. Forgetful. Stubborn. Moody. The list of descriptors goes on and on. Do you really believe your child is born with all the strengths and skills she needs to be the perfect child and simply refuses to behave well?

Tucker is a seventeen-year-old who frequently borrows his mother's car. At first he used the car just to go back and forth to work. Every so often he would ask to borrow the car to go out with friends. His mother, single and hard working, told him he could use her car as long as he agreed to take great care of it since it's her only way to get to work. He needed to be home by eleven and never drink when he drove. Tucker agreed to this fence.

In the beginning, Tucker followed the rules expecting his mother would enforce them. But each time he came home, the door was unlocked, the lights dimmed and his mother in bed for the night. Soon, Tucker came home when he pleased and often drove after having a few beers; after all, who would know? It wasn't until he pushed the fence one too many times that Tucker's mother found out what he was really doing. She was angry with Tucker because he disregarded her rules. She was frustrated with herself for believing tell-me discipline would be enough to help Tucker make good decisions. She felt put out; now she'd have to stay up later than she should given she worked an early morning shift.

The popular assumption that a child prefers to push fences rather than accept them is flat out wrong. Fences get pushed for so many reasons. Your child's fence pushing is complicated. Blaming parents isn't going to change how fences are built and reinforced. Blaming your child won't work either.

Your child isn't right or wrong, good or bad. Tucker isn't a perfect child; no such child exists. His story simply illustrates that all behavior tells a story. Remember those three factors that shape the parenting experience. Tucker's story, and your child's, too, highlights how behavior is influenced by your parenting style, his temperament, and your family's lifestyle.

With compassionate understanding of your child's temperament, you'll be able to appreciate who your child is, and learn to choose the right tell-me, show-me discipline. In this section, I'll delve deeper into the second factor that affects your parenting experience: your child's style or temperament. You'll learn about who pushes fences and why. Then you'll take the second of the three quizzes, this one aimed at helping you understand your child's temperament.

In the Yard or Through the Gate

Every parent wants to know how much a child's success in life depends on the way he's parented and how much success depends on innate traits. Is the successful child born or made? The nature-nurture argument is a debate that's raged on for years and one that's certain to continue. There's really no need to debate which predictive factors lead to success, because both do. Nature, or your child's biology, plays a strong role in how your child will behave. And the way your child is nurtured by you plays a strong role in how your child will behave.

Your parenting style has a lot to do with whether or not your child will push fences. If you waver, your child will look high and low for the fences you've hidden or failed to build. If you react, your child will push each and every fence you build, looking for the freedom you've failed to offer.

After examining your parenting style, first by taking the quiz "Are You a Proactive Parent?" and then reading the chapters in Part II, you've got a much better idea where your strengths are for parenting and what you might want to fine-tune in your approach to communicating the behavior that is negotiable and that which is not.

Whether you're already proactive or working on becoming more proactive, your style is only one factor on the nurture side of the nature-nurture equation. The choices you make for your child such as when she eats, how much she sleeps, and in how many activities she participates are just a few of the lifestyle factors that will contribute to how she behaves. Your parenting style and your lifestyle together make up the external or environmental factors that influence your child's behavior. Nurture.

Nature. Your son loves jazz music. Your daughter loves classical. And you like peace and quiet. Certainly you can teach each child to appreciate the other's favorite music but you won't be able to change his passion for blues or her enthusiasm for symphonies. Your child's biology is very predictive of the way she'll respond to your fences. Her likes and dislikes, her way of doing things is hard-wired into her from head to toe. You won't be able to change her hard-wiring but you will be able to teach your child the skills she needs to manage the aspects of her biology that work for her and those that make life more challenging. Being proactive is all about changing the skills; but first you'll need to understand the hard-wiring.

It's in the Bag

Every child has behavioral strengths. Your child may be kind and sensitive to the needs of others. Or your child may stick with a new challenge no matter how hard. Or your child may dive into new learning experiences.

I'd like you to imagine your child holding an invisible bag by her side. In this bag, your child holds her strengths for managing the situations she confronts alone and with others. If you have more than one child, each of their bags holds different skills, different strengths.

The shy child may play well alone but have difficulty playing with others; she has self-entertaining skills in her bag but lacks certain social skills. The outgoing child may play well with others but have difficulty sharing toys; he has social skills in his bag, but struggles with cooperation skills. In order to parent effectively you'll need to identify each of your child's strengths as well as determine which skills each child still needs to learn. Identifying the skills your child still needs to develop is the first step in helping your child put the new and necessary skills in the bag.

Charlotte is an eleven-year-old sixth grader who is responsible for practically every social gathering at her middle school. She organizes car washes and movie nights. She puts out flyers and makes phone calls to be sure as many students as possible attend these social events. She's been chosen by friends and teachers alike as the student with the most school spirit. No one could argue that Charlotte's bag isn't overflowing with social skills. Effective communication skills, friendship skills, organizational skills; they're all in the bag.

Charlotte's bag is not filled with the same vast array of skills for academic success. She struggles particularly in math and science. Studying for long periods of time alone isn't something she's motivated to do. The concepts in both subjects are dry and uninteresting to her. Without interaction from her peers, Charlotte sees studying for these subjects as nothing short of torture. Charlotte has strengths. Charlotte has skills to build. This is the case with every child's bag. Knowing what's already in Charlotte's bag or your child's bag will help everyone maximize strengths and fill the bag with necessary skills to increase success in every area.

Three building blocks are found in every child's bag and you'll need to understand each one if you're going to add to your child's behavioral repertoire in any positive or meaningful way. These building blocks are your child's development, temperament, and behavioral skills.

Development refers to your child's *capability* to behave. As your child matures, she can do more and learn more. Temperament refers to your child's *style* of behavior. Every child is uniquely hardwired and comes by her behavioral strengths and struggles naturally. Behavioral skills refer to *how well* your child can already behave in certain situations. These skills are learned through repeated experiences both positive and negative.

Brothers Miguel, five, and Jordie, nine, are going to be attendants in their aunt Joyce's wedding. The boys' mother tries to explain to her sister, Joyce, how important it will be to keep expectations low and preparation high for both boys but especially for nine-year-old Jordie.

"Joyce, I know you think whatever the boys do is cute. But this wedding is going to be hard for them. Miguel is pretty mellow most of the time but he's going to have a really hard time paying attention, especially in church. And you know Jordie; he can't sit still for more than ten minutes. I'm afraid he'll be running down the aisle making a scene. Talking with adults they hardly ever see and taking all those pictures, I'm a wreck just thinking about it."

"Miguel's young. People will think he's adorable. And come on, Jordie's nine, for goodness sake. He's old enough to behave if we tell him how important it is to me. He'll be fine; he's the oldest."

Two boys, two different bags. And age is only part of it. The boys' mother knows that although Miguel is typically easygoing, being a wedding attendant is still asking a lot of a five-year-old. Her concerns for Jordie center on his temperament. Though Jordie is the older of the boys, he is active, social, and often acts impulsively in new situations. This mother knows her boys' bags. She realizes each boy has different abilities to behave, different styles for behaving, and different skills already in their bags. She's right to be examining whether or not their bags have what it takes to be successful at the wedding. Knowing their strengths along with what skills they'll need, she can prevent predictable issues and prepare the boys for what will be expected.

The same expectations, but two different boys with very different behavior. In order to build the right fences, you must understand what's in the bag and what still needs to be added.

Do you know what's in your child's bag?

Birthdays and Breakthroughs

In living rooms and on playgrounds, mothers and fathers can't resist learning about development by putting their child up against another child of the same age. It's tempting to compare one child with another in an attempt to learn what your child should be capable of at his age, what should be in the bag.

"When did your baby sleep through the night?" "How old was your son when he was finally potty trained?" "My four-year-old is reading, is yours?" "Boys, put your backs together and we'll see who's taller."

Every parent does it; it's one way to learn about development. If you know what your child should be doing at each developmental age, it helps you know what you can hold your child accountable for. Some expectations are clearer than others. You can expect two-year-olds to communicate with words and body language. Six-year-olds go to school, and seventeen-year-olds learn to drive. While there will always be exceptions—a child may not have or ever develop certain skills—but in most cases developmental expectations are clear cut, they don't present any confusion. Other milestones based on age are far more puzzling: Shouldn't my child have more friends? When should my child be able to do homework on his own? Is my child ready to stay home alone? And the list goes on.

If you ask me questions about development, I'll need two bits of information to answer your question appropriately. If you want to know about walking, for example, the first thing I need to know is the wide range of normal for the developmental milestone you're asking about. The normal age range for a child learning to walk is anywhere from nine months to fifteen months.

The second thing I need to know is how old your child is. If you tell me your child is ten months old and not yet interested in pulling himself to a standing position, I'll tell you to relax and enjoy the simplicity of supervising your nonwalker. But if you tell me your child is sixteen months old and not interested in any way, I'll tell you it's time to talk to your pediatrician. Your child might be a slow walker or there might be a developmental reason for his lack of interest in learning this skill.

When your child has a breakthrough in learning a new skill, she's reached what's called a developmental milestone. The wide range of normal for a certain skill *plus* your child's age is far more meaningful than your child's age alone. Does every child learn to write his letters by his fifth birthday? No. All skills are learned at your child's own pace, in her own time.

Can you enhance, encourage, and aid your child's learning? Of course, but you won't be able to teach or coach your child to learn a new skill if you disregard the beginning point of the wide range of normal for a skill. Would you attempt to teach a three-month-old child to write her name with a pencil? Would you teach a three-year-old child to fly a plane? Teaching a child these skills for which he or she doesn't have developmental readiness would be a waste of time for both of you.

Use information about development as one of your tools for effective parenting. First, find the range of normal for a skill or task by reading or talking to development experts such as your child's pediatrician or his teacher. Second, learn what's already in your child's bag for developmental readiness.

Comparing your child to others might be appealing but it's not always the best way to get an accurate sense of what your child can or should be doing. There's a new and disturbing movement toward parents and educators seeing a few children, for whom certain skills come easy, and then applying this new yardstick to all children.

When an inaccurate developmental benchmark is applied, it makes a child who may be slower to learn a skill or skills appear atypical, abnormal, or developmentally delayed when she is not. Remember, your child will learn in her own way, in due time. You can always facilitate learning but you shouldn't try to rush or push it. And don't compare; measure your child's success by her own standard, not by the development of another child.

All learning is a personal experience and when your child experiences a breakthrough both you and she will know it. So look into your child's bag; respect her unique strengths and capabilities to learn. Childhood is a journey, not a race.

A Mixed Bag

I'm an early riser, I have a passion for books, and I can't bear the sound of dogs barking when I'm writing. My best friend is a night owl, loves to travel, and hates sand in his shoes. Who are you? What do you love? What bothers you most? Do you choose these preferences or do they choose you?

Hard-wiring. Biological map. Inborn traits. It doesn't matter which label you choose, your child's temperament is evident early on. The way your child eats, sleeps, and plays tells you a lot about his nature. Many people hear the word *temperament* and mistake it for the word *temperamental*. These two words are very different. Temperament is a word that refers to biologically based patterns of behavior. Everyone has a temperament. Temperamental is a judgmental word that implies a person's hard-wiring is bad or hard to deal with. I'm going to use the word *temperament* and steer clear of the word *temperamental*, because it's inappropriate to blame any child for his or her biological nature.

Many people hear the word temperament and mistake it for the word temperamental. These two words are very different.

Every child moves his body—activity level. If you have a very active child you might at times find his behavior challenging. Every child has her own way of managing change and handling the unexpected—adaptability level. But if you have a child who hates change and simply can't go with the flow, you might find her behavior challenging at times, too.

It's helpful to look at temperament in terms of nine traits, often called elements of temperament. These elements of temperament, found in every child's bag, vary in the degrees in which they're present. But remember everyone, including you, has all nine.

Activity: your child's level of movement and energy

Adaptability: your child's ability to adjust to change, transitions and the unexpected

Distractibility: your child's level of attention and ability to dismiss distractions

Intensity: your child's pattern of reacting to feelings and everyday situations

Mood: your child's state of mind and general outlook

Persistence: your child's ability to persevere to accomplish a task or meet a goal

Physical regularity: your child's patterns of eating, sleeping, and eliminating

Reactivity: your child's pattern of approaching something or someone new

Sensitivity: your child's ability to feel both physically and emotionally

Do you have one child who is less sensitive to her sister's feelings and one who is more? The child who exhibits less of a trait, say sensitivity, will need to learn to be more concerned about the feelings of those around her. Your other child will need little coaching from you to learn this because she's already hard-wired to be sensitive. Or maybe you have one child who remembers things with precision and one who forgets everything you say. The highly focused child won't need your help to remember things but your other child will need your coaching to learn how to focus his attention.

The elements of temperament found in your child's bag may make it easy for her to behave well or it may make life more challenging for her. Whatever the case, what's in her bag is who she is; not right or wrong, good or bad. Just her.

Victoria storms through the back door, tosses her backpack on the floor, and says, "It's official. I hate fifth grade." She proceeds to tell her dad all the horrible things that happened to her on this her first day of school.

"My teacher yells. I don't have any friends in my class. And at lunch, you're not allowed to sit with another class. And there's going to be way too much homework. It's going to be an awful year. Yesterday, I was a kid with recess and today I'm a kid with responsibilities."

Wow. Victoria is articulate and Victoria is intense. She feels things deeply. She adapts to change by expressing her feelings with vivid language and dramatic gestures. Victoria has never been described by her parents as mellow. She was born with this temperament, and she won't wake up one day and suddenly go with the flow. Like Victoria, your child's style of behaving is biological and stable over time.

Hard-wiring defines how a child will respond to her environment and to your fences. You won't be able to change your child's hard-wiring but with a proactive—not reactive—approach to skill-building you can enhance, refine, and modify the skills your child has for behaving well. Sometimes strong elements of temperament, such as intensity or persistence, interfere with your child's ability to accept fences and enjoy the freedom found in the backyard. But you can predict behavior based on your child's development *and* his temperament.

A typical three-year-old might get out of bed when he should be sleeping, as does any persistent child. A typical thirteen-year-old may get her feelings hurt easily, as does any sensitive child. The elements of temperament found in your child's bag help you to predict behavior. Is your child's temperament likely to produce a lot of fence pushing? It's time to take the next quiz and see.

Is your child a fence pusher?

— —

This quiz is intended to give you insight into the temperament elements that influence how likely your child is to push boundaries or limits. It is best to take the quiz for one child at a time.

DIRECTIONS

For each item below, circle how accurately this statement describes your child.

A = Very accurate
B = Accurate
C = Not accurate

1. Strives for independence	A	B	C ✓
2. Is a black-and-white thinker	A	B ✓	C
3. Loves to be in charge	A	B ✓	C
4. Can be impulsive	A	B	C ✓

5. Is stubborn or relentless when she   A   B ✓   C
   wants something

6. Is always moving; has difficulty   A   B   C ✓
   slowing down

7. Talks a lot   A   B   C ✓

8. Is curious; asks a lot of questions   A   B ✓   C

9. Is a risk-taker or thrill-seeker   A   B   C ✓

10. Is rigid and inflexible   A   B   C ✓

11. Learns by doing; is a hands-on learner   A ✓   B   C

12. Takes things literally   A ✓   B   C

13. Loves change   A ✓   B   C

14. Has strong desires   A   B ✓   C

15. Is very optimistic   A   B ✓   C

16. Can be anxious or moody   A   B ✓   C

17. Is creative or artistic   A   B   C ✓

18. Makes friends easily   A   B ✓   C

19. Learns things quickly   A   B ✓   C

20. Is more concerned with finishing a task   A   B   C ✓
    than with the quality of the work

The Results

Now add up how many As, Bs, and Cs you circled. Identify the
letter you chose most often and then look at the corresponding
description below. The description will highlight how much your

child's temperament sets him or her up for fence pushing, and will guide you as you factor this information into your parenting. Remember, your child will require individualized discipline strategies based on his or her unique temperament.

MOSTLY As   *The Dynamic Style*

Your child has a number of strong elements of temperament. In light of this, you definitely need to strategize with temperament in mind. Your child will benefit from discipline that factors in how he reacts to the people and events around him. You play a key role in maximizing your child's strengths and teaching him the skills he needs to accept fences in ways that are less stressful for both of you. Being proactive is critical to your parenting success with the dynamic child.

MOSTLY Bs   *The Situational Style*

Your child has some strong elements of temperament that impact her ability to accept fences, and other factors that contribute to her understanding of rules. The key to parenting the child with the situational style is to strategize with temperament in mind, when certain predictable situations occur in which your child often has difficulty. It will be important for you to consider how her temperament and complex situations come together to make accepting fences hard for her. Being proactive means anticipating where and when your child will need your coaching. Both you and your child will benefit from looking at themes in tough situations.

MOSTLY Cs   *The Agreeable Style*

Your child has few elements of temperament that could be considered strong. You probably find this child easy to parent because of his ability to adapt easily to your fences. Factoring temperament into your parenting may feel less crucial, but it's always important to build good fences. While your child may be easy to parent because of his ability to go with flow, he may be lacking important skills that could benefit him as he learns to get his needs met. Your child's behavior doesn't have to be disruptive for him to benefit from the proactive strategies found in this approach.

Test the Waters

Your child's temperament helps you predict how much fence pushing you can expect. Whether your child has a number of strong elements of temperament or very few, if you can predict the degree to which there will be fence pushing, you can be prepared for it. The dynamic child will push more than the situational child. The situational child will push more than the agreeable child. But don't forget, *every child* will push fences more if you waver or react, or if your lifestyle is geared more toward your traits than your child's.

Some parents see a lot of fence pushing and instead of thinking it's related to a child's nature or temperament, wonder if something more might be going on. Do you worry that your child is so distractible that he has attention deficit disorder? Could your child's moodiness mean he's depressed? Keep in mind, just because he routinely demonstrates an inability to accept fences, it doesn't necessarily mean his behavior indicates a particular diagnosis.

> *Don't forget, every child will push fences more if you waver or react, or if your lifestyle is geared more toward your traits than your child's.*

More often than not, behavioral issues are related to your child's temperament or the way stress exaggerates his patterns of behavior. There has been a disturbing trend toward parents and teachers wondering if every dreamy student has attention deficit disorder and every moody teenager, depression. It bears repeating: Behavioral issues are first and foremost temperament related. And temperament can appear more extreme when your child is experiencing stress at home or at school.

Stop and think about what makes your child's existing patterns of behavior more challenging. How does your child behave when she gets a cold or you have a new baby? Or when Nana is visiting or Dad's on a business trip? Perhaps she struggles at the holidays or when the seasons change. All of these typical life events affect behavior and can exaggerate an already strong temperament.

Though it may be tempting to get swept along with the current trend to see your child's fence-pushing behavior as a diagnosis or disorder, I want you to test the behavioral waters by casting a small net first. When it comes to your child's behavior, the simplest explanation is likely to be the best. First, assume your child's behavior is temperament related. By using the techniques I describe throughout the book, you may find that all your child needs is better fences, ones built around her temperament.

Distinguishing between temperament and a behavioral diagnosis is complicated even for a trained professional. The best professionals will refrain from leaping to a behavioral diagnosis before more simple measures—like a proactive plan—have been implemented and evaluated. If you adopt a proactive approach and behavior doesn't improve or if your child has already been diagnosed with a behavioral condition, then by all means pursue additional complementary strategies for managing your child's behavioral issues such as medical and/or mental health intervention.

If you're unsure whether your child's behavioral issues are diagnostic in nature, be sure to consult a trained professional, someone who can guide you through the process of diagnosing and treating your child's possible behavioral condition appropriately. Please keep in mind, even if your child's behavior is related to a particular diagnosis, learn about temperament and be proactive, because every child deserves solid and predictable fences.

Pack Your Child's Bag

All behavior tells a story. There's always a reason you do what you do. Regardless of the *why* behind your child's behavior, you can fill his bag with new skills, smooth out ineffective ones, and celebrate those that consistently work well for him. Every child's bag has it all: the good, the not so good, and the great. While you might find it easier to tell others what you love about your child, you might find it harder to tell your child. Energy in parenting is often spent focused on what your child does wrong instead of what your child does right.

Finn is a fourteen-year-old cross-country runner. He runs long distances with passion and heart. He entered a regional competition and won first place in his age category. On cloud nine, he returns home after a long day and tells his mother about the award. She's pleased and congratulates him on his accomplishment. The next morning when Finn is getting ready for school, he can't seem to find his science book. He realizes he left it on the bus that brought him home from the competition. His mother spends the rest of the morning lecturing Finn on how irresponsible he is when it comes to anything other than his running.

Finn can run. Finn is disorganized. But his mother's lecturing and nagging will never change his bag. When Finn gets older, he might get better at juggling his responsibilities. But it's possible he'll never fully learn to balance every aspect of his life.

Some behavior gets better on its own; repeated exposure and lots of experience do the teaching. Finn might need to lose his science book, his English book, and finally his math book before he learns how to keep track of his belongings.

Most behavior gets better with good fences and even better follow-through. Finn's mother can put new skills in her child's bag through an active process of teaching him how to be organized, a planned approach to tell-me, show-me discipline.

Will you take your chances and hope your child learns to behave differently because he's older and wiser and he's been exposed to the natural results of his actions or inaction? Will you hope life experience teaches him enough valuable lessons to change his ways? Or will you proactively build skill with exposure and experience so he'll grow up with a bag rich in skills for good decision-making, truly shaping his character?

There is a third option, of course. No learning takes place at all; his bag remains unchanged. Your child doesn't choose to learn through exposure and experience, and you choose not to skill-build. If this is your choice, your child who doesn't have the skills now grows up to be an adult who doesn't have the skills.

Clearly the optimal approach is to skill-build to give your child the tools he needs in his bag. Let me show you how.

9. Why Skill-Building Works Better Than Time-Outs, Grounding, and Take-Aways

Cathryn clutches her driver's manual in one hand and the car keys in the other. Today will be her first time behind the wheel of her father's car. She took her learner's permit test; she passed. She's started her classroom hours in a driver's education program run by her school. She's read, talked, and thought about driving for weeks but she's nervous. With her father's guidance, Cathryn will put her new knowledge about driving to the test.

She walks to the car, puts her hand on the door handle, and freezes. "What if I can't do it? What if I get into an accident the first time I drive?"

Her father places a reassuring hand on her shoulder. "Cathryn, you're not going to start right here, right now. We're going to an empty parking lot where you'll be able to get a feel for driving. You'll have a chance to learn where all the instruments are, like turn signals, windshield wipers, and defrost controls. This is just your first time out. You'll need to relax and have realistic expectations. You're not going to be a pro by the end of the morning. But you're going to do just fine. I'll help you learn to be a great driver."

Manuals and permit tests are examples of tell-me teaching and learning. Parking lots and road tests are examples of show-me teaching and learning. New skills are learned with exposure to both kinds of teaching. Certainly Cathryn's father will *tell her* what he expects her to do: Park between the lines. Use side and rearview mirrors. No radio, for now. And certainly he'll need to *show her* tricks for parking between the lines and how to use the mirrors. Perhaps he'll even have to turn off the radio should her first successful experience lead to overconfidence.

Tell-me, show-me teaching and learning. Discipline. What do you think or feel when you consider that word? Many parents leap to the notion a child has done something wrong. "He needs more discipline." "Someone ought to discipline that girl." The word *discipline*, for many, is synonymous with the word *punishment*. But will Cathryn's father punish her if she forgets to use her turn signals or parks out of the marked lines in the parking lot?

When you're helping to build thinking skills like reading or multiplication, it's clear that punishment would be an inappropriate and even destructive way to get reading or math skills in the bag. Practice is key. There are behavioral skills where most everyone realizes punishment would be inappropriate, such as when you train your child to use the toilet, or teach your child to ride a bike, or drive a car. Yet when it comes to other behavior skills like staying in bed, completing a science project, or coming home in time for dinner, many see punishment as the only way to get new or different skills for behaving in the bag. Why not assume if your child could do those things he would? He just needs someone to teach him how. And he needs to practice.

Punishment Is a Crime

Andy shoves Zack trying to get the last cookie. You wouldn't call it attempted robbery. Anita hits Zinny with a softball to get her out of the game. You wouldn't call it assault with a deadly weapon. These behaviors are unacceptable, it's true. But your child's inappropriate and ineffective behavior doesn't constitute criminal acts punishable by confinement otherwise known as time-outs and grounding. Or punishable by the payment of penalties and fees otherwise known as consequences and take-aways. Even judges and jurors rarely yell at the accused.

You can choose to spend your time reacting. You can punish behavior that is developmentally expected or the result of your child's biological hard-wiring; behavior that is quite often predictable. Or you can teach your child how to do things differently. You can put new skills in the bag.

Ten-year-old Eva has her own room. She enjoys decorating the walls with posters of her favorite contestants from *American Idol.* She moves the furniture around every month, or so it seems to Eva's mother, Margot. The one thing Eva doesn't enjoy doing to her room is cleaning it.

Margot tries to change Eva's behavior with punishment. "Eva, I've had it. Your room's a mess and I want you to clean it on Saturday. If you choose not to, there will be consequences. Do you understand?"

Eva, busy reading a teen magazine, looks up at her mother and says, "Yeah, I know, I need to clean my room."

Did Eva clean her room? Or did Margot dish out those consequences? You guessed correctly if you imagined Saturday came and went. Sunday, Margot went to check Eva's room, found it messy, and started to take away cherished items and favorite privileges in an effort to make her point: Clean your room.

"That's it. I'm taking away *Idol* this week and you're not going to stay after school tomorrow for chorus. You've got to take responsibility for your room. We've been fighting about this for a year. If I've told you once, I've told you a hundred times: Clean your room. I mean it."

Is anything working with Margot's current approach? She's doing a lot of talking about something supposedly nonnegotiable and Eva's room is still a mess. By taking away television and chorus, which don't relate to the cleaning expectation, Eva's behavior related to cleaning her room is unlikely to change. This ongoing battle between Margot and her daughter surfaces at least once a month and has for the last year. Margot has used tell-me discipline—a hundred times—yet this behavioral theme continues. Isn't spending time in your room doing lots of things, with little if any time spent cleaning, typical behavior for a ten-year-old? If you can predict it, you can prevent it.

There is another way. Margot can try to change Eva's behavior with skill-building. "Eva, on Friday I'm going to buy some plastic bins, shelves, and a hamper. Saturday, I'm going to show you how I expect your room to look. You can choose what you want to put in the bins and on the shelves but by the end of the day your room will be clean."

"Can we move the furniture around, too?"

"First, you'll need to clean it. Then we can talk about moving furniture."

Margot built a nonnegotiable fence: The room needs to be cleaned. She's also offered freedom within the backyard in the form of bins and shelves. She's offered direction and it sounds like she'll be there to guide the process, too.

Later Saturday afternoon, Eva's room is clean and she is pleased, as is Margot. Now Margot will need to build a different fence for keeping the room clean. One that will include tell-me discipline. Perhaps she'll tell Eva—before the room is a mess again—clothes go in the hamper, books on the shelves and her bed needs to be made each morning. Her plan will need to include show-me discipline, too. Perhaps the expectation is that Eva does those three things before leaving for school. How will Margot ensure her expectation isn't all talk and no action? She'll need to check Eva's room to see if she's done these three things before she goes to school. If Eva forgets or tests the limit, Margot can walk her daughter to her room and simply point to the three things. Again, if this expectation is not negotiable—the talking is over.

Are you thinking that Eva is capable of cleaning her room, she simply chooses not to? This question assumes Margot's value of having a clean room is a value equally held by her daughter. Remember the bag. Eva is ten with limited experience cleaning and being responsible for her belongings. She may be hard-wired to be somewhat disorganized, lacking skills for keeping things tidy. She'll need repeated exposure and lots of experience cleaning the room before it's an automatic behavior. She'll need tell-me and show-me discipline to go together, consistently, so she can accept this non-negotiable fence. But if the expectations are too high or the follow-through inconsistent, she'll still have difficulty accepting the fence for cleaning her room.

Don't make the mistake of measuring what's in your child's bag by looking in your own. Just because your child may be physically capable of doing a task once or even more than once doesn't mean she can do it all the time and without you there to reinforce the fence. Your fences will be only as good as your willingness to make them real via follow-through. You won't always have to follow through, but you must always be willing to do so.

Punishment only leads to more punishment. Skill-building leads to better and stronger skills. How long do you think it took Eva to get the message her room will need to stay clean? The answer depends on three things. First, she must recognize a relationship between an action and a reaction, the tell-me, show-me connection. Skill-building is rounded out when Eva experiences her mother's follow-through often enough to believe her mother will follow through each and every time Eva pushes a fence. Then and only then does the skill go in the bag and behavior become automatic; your child learns self-discipline. One day Margot walked into Eva's room and found it clean without having had to say or do anything to make it so.

Punishment only leads to more punishment. Skill-building leads to better and stronger skills.

Putting on a Life Jacket

Your child learns every time he makes a connection between one thing and another. If you say "Brush your teeth," as you hand your child his toothbrush, he gets the message it's time to brush his teeth. If you say "Play in the driveway," and then you walk your son up the driveway whenever he comes too close to the street, he gets the message he must play in the driveway. *Connections. If I do this, that will happen. Action with predictable reactions.*

Eighteen-month-old Carrie has a new habit. She stands up in her high chair. Her mother, Nan, is becoming increasingly concerned for her safety. Today, Nan decides she'll take Carrie out of the high chair every time she stands up. Before the next time she puts her daughter in the high chair, she says, "You'll sit down in your high chair and you'll eat." That's it. She doesn't say, "Don't do this or if you do this, I'll do that." She keeps it simple.

At first, Carrie ate. Then Carrie stood up. And Nan respectfully but matter-of-factly took her out. Carrie gestured to her mother to put her back into the high chair. Nan did so and guess what? Carrie stood up. Nan took her out again and this time the meal was over. Nan wasn't focused on punishing her daughter or taking away the opportunity to eat. Nan was teaching Carrie about mealtime expectations.

At first, Carrie thought this was a game; she was learning cause and effect with no judgment related to whether she should or shouldn't be doing this. Learning right from wrong is a sophisticated skill more solidly in the older child's bag. She was simply learning if she does this, that will happen. And she wants to be sure she's figured it out. At the next meal, Nan finds Carrie has clearly received the message she's been teaching. If she wants to eat, she'll need to sit down. The new skill has been placed in the bag. How did Nan know the learning had taken place? The next time Carrie stood up in her high chair, Nan got out of her own chair to walk over to the high chair to take Carrie out, and Carrie quickly sat down. A connection had been made because Nan had been consistent. Each time her daughter stood up, she took her out. With this consistently taught connection, Carrie became certain of Nan's next move.

Like Carrie, your child is making associations between the things you say and the things you do, all the time. The bad news is some of the connections your child's making are between things you'd rather not get connected.

If you tell your son he needs to mow the lawn and then you mow it yourself, he learns he doesn't really need to do the chores you tell him to do. I call this a faulty connection. You may not have wanted to teach him this connection, but you did.

The good news is some of the connections he's making are healthy ones. You tell your son he needs to mow the lawn but he doesn't come home from his friend's house to do it. You get in your car and drive over to his friend's to get him. Now he's learned your expectation to mow the lawn is real.

Your power lies in helping your child to make healthy connections. If you fear your child has already made some faulty connections, take heart: When you become more consistent in making positive healthy connections, your child will become certain your tell-me discipline and your show-me discipline *will* go together.

Timmy loves sailing with his dad, Sean. And Sean loves sailing with seven-year-old Timmy. Though Sean follows many important safety rules aboard his boat, he rarely—if ever—makes Timmy wear his life jacket. Following a boating accident involving friends, Sean has decided the time has come for Timmy to follow the rule.

Sean realizes he's taught Timmy a faulty connection; the rule is you must wear the life jacket, but you really don't need to follow it. In order to change behavior, Sean must first predict that Timmy will assign the faulty connection to the new expectation. After all, the rule wasn't really a rule before. Sean will need to prepare Timmy to accept the new fence. And he'll need to consistently follow through with the new expectation. The rule becomes real when Sean shows his son he must wear the jacket. He can delay starting the boat until the jacket is on or he can hand Timmy the jacket. But he'll need to help Timmy make the new connection with consistency, so Timmy will be certain Sean means what he says.

If Sean follows through this weekend but not next, he's still teaching Timmy rules change like the wind. In order to make new skills get in the bag and stay there, Sean will need to teach the new connection and be consistent in his expectation. Only then will Timmy be certain Sean will do as he says. Timmy will put the jacket on, time and time again, because that's just what young boaters do.

What does Timmy learn when Sean consistently follows through on this rule? He doesn't just learn to wear the life jacket. He also learns to respect safety rules in general and his father's authority specifically.

When faulty connections have already been made, you can disconnect them by making healthy connections with consistency and certainty. Once you teach your child positive healthy connections, these skills are in the bag for good, for a lifetime.

Parents as Teachers

Let's talk about what's in your child's bag. Skills for cleaning her room, mowing the lawn, or being safe on a boat? It's up to you. I want you to move away from seeing yourself as disciplinarian, a word that conjures up images of punishment. I want you to move toward an image of you as your child's teacher. One who knows the new skills required. One who plans what will be taught and how. And someone who holds her child accountable for what's been taught. Yes, there will be a test. It's called life.

You want your child to behave well now for many reasons. You want your child to have opportunities to learn great things, to make good friends, and to enjoy healthy relationships with teachers and coaches. And you want to enjoy a happy, meaningful, and respectful relationship with your child, too. Your short-term goals aimed at nurturing effective behavior are valuable, but what's even more important is recognizing that right this very minute, you're shaping the adult your child will become.

> *I want you to move away from seeing yourself as disciplinarian, a word that conjures up images of punishment. I want you to move toward an image of you as your child's teacher.*

When you see your role of parent as teacher, you're in a powerful position to fill your child's bag with great skills, ones he'll certainly need now but ones that later will turn out to be vital for succeeding in the world.

What would you like to teach? So much is possible. Start with something you'll be successful teaching, something small and uncomplicated. When you experience the process of skill-building with your child and the new skill goes in the bag, both of you experience the benefits of this approach. You'll have predicted and prepared your child for your new expectation and your child will acquire a new skill. At first, one skill is just one skill. Soon, all the skills will accumulate and your child will make new connections quickly, becoming more certain of your overall expectations for behavior. She'll become self-disciplined about what is negotiable and what is not.

Teaching any new skill begins with preparation. Every teacher has a lesson plan. The first and most important question you'll need to ask is whether or not your child has the developmental capability to learn the skill you'd like to teach.

Vera wants to teach Cole to put away his coat and school bag when he gets home each afternoon. Sounds like a good skill to have, doesn't it? If I tell you Cole is sixteen, you'd expect it's high time he learn this skill. In your mind, Cole is more than capable. If I tell you Cole is one, you'd probably think it's a bit premature to teach this skill; his developmental capability isn't likely in the bag quite yet. But if I tell you Cole is three, you might look at the tell-me, show-me discipline required in a different light. Cole could be successful with a coat hook rather than a coat hanger and if the hook is low rather than high. Your child's developmental capability will guide what you teach, when you teach, and how your child will learn.

The second and equally important question you'll ask relates to your child's temperament. Will your child's unique hard-wiring facilitate the learning or make it more challenging? You simply can't dismiss the role your child's hard-wiring has on learning. If Cole is easily distracted, teaching the new skill will not only take longer but you'll need to be prepared to follow through more often, walking him to his coat so he can hang it up. If Cole is slow to adapt to change, he may resist learning the new skill because he'll prefer you continue to hang up his coat and bag. Asking critical questions about your child's temperament along with his development will help you to create the right tell-me, show-me strategies you'll need to get the new skills in the bag.

Mack and Mabel are five-year-old twins, as different as night and day. The children's parents would like to begin going to religious services as a family. Going to Mass will require skills for sitting still, being quiet, waiting patiently, and participating appropriately. These are sophisticated skills for many five-year-olds; some might say for some adults, too.

The plan to build skills begins with looking at Mack's and Mabel's developmental capabilities. Mabel is a typically developing five-year-old; she's reached development milestones for talking, walking, and socializing earlier than some her age. Mack's speech is delayed and he tends to be hesitant to leave his parents' side. Socializing is hard for him.

Next, look at the temperament of each child. Which traits will make skill-building easy and which might make skill-building hard? Mabel is physically active and eager to meet new people and try new things. Mack doesn't like bright lights and loud noises. He tends to become clingy when faced with meeting new people or joining new groups.

Can both learn the skills needed to be successful in church? Certainly they can. But the children's parents will need to predict the potential trouble spots for each child and prepare them individually for the options available to them for behaving well.

Predict and prevent. Predict and prepare. Mack's and Mabel's parents have a number of options for skill-building. They could choose to skill-build one child at a time. Once one child is successful in church, they could begin skill-building with the next child. Or each parent could prepare one child, taking each to a separate

Mass. Or they could skill-build as a family, talking together about church; what will it be like and what will be expected? Regardless of which approach they take to begin skill-building, each child will benefit from lots of practice.

Training sessions, run-throughs, rehearsals—vicarious experience. Whatever you call it, whichever term you prefer, every child acquires skills faster and more effectively the more opportunity he has to practice. Anyone want to play church?

Child's Play

Play is your child's natural language. Playing house. Playing school. Playing hospital. These childhood games teach your child rules for living, techniques for learning, and ways of coping with what life sends in her direction. Never underestimate the power of play. Play isn't kid stuff; you're never too old to play.

Violet is twelve and eager to begin babysitting. She's taken a class at the local community center and can't wait for the opportunity to work. Today is her lucky day. Cora, Violet's mother, meets her at the back door after school with good news.

"Violet, Mrs. Dunn called and she'd like you to be her mother's helper after school on Fridays. I met her last week at the market and told her you'd taken the babysitting course. She'd like you to call her back today so you can discuss the details."

"Mom, what do I say? I really want the job but I don't know what to say."

"That's okay. I'll practice with you before you call her. There are certain things she'll definitely ask you and you'll be ready with your answers."

Role-playing is a wonderful way to teach skill. When your child is young, you can play restaurant or school to show your child what your expectations are. But when your child is older, role-playing is the verbal equivalent and equally effective in teaching skill. Haven't you practiced a speech or rehearsed for a job interview?

When you're proactive in skill-building, you anticipate the situations in which your child, younger or older, would benefit from practicing in advance. With play or role-play, the real situation is less stressful and the new skills easier to pull out of the bag when they're needed.

Parents as Coaches

A good coach brings out the best in each player. First, he teaches strategies aimed at winning the game and then expects each player to use them. When a player can't seem to get the hang of a particular play, the coach recognizes the need for more practice. Perhaps he'll add some training sessions or encourage the player to practice every chance he gets. Yet during a real game, a good coach uses gestures from the sidelines to remind the player what he wants him to do, or he might choose to pull a player to the bench to review the play before the next time he goes in.

Some coaches scream and yell from the sidelines or take players out of the game entirely. But that doesn't teach the player how to use the strategy any better. If a coach really wants a player to perform better, this just isn't the right response. You can't learn to play any better if you're not in the game.

I'm sure you've heard the word *consequences* as it relates to parenting. Maybe you subscribe to the thinking that your child should feel the negative consequences of his actions. You might want to know the specific consequences to attach to certain behaviors. For many, just like the word *discipline*, the word *consequences* conjures up thoughts of finding the right punishment to fit the crime. If you want to be the kind of coach that doesn't play the blame game, I invite you to disregard the notion of consequences and start using the RITE response.

The RITE response involves responding to behavior in ways that are *respectful, infraction-based, timely,* and *effective.* Instead of trying to find a penalty to fit a crime, you'll create fences in advance and then use the RITE response to remind your child the fence is indeed real.

Respectful responses to misbehavior never include yelling, shouting, or demeaning your child. You wouldn't want your boss to teach you a new software program or a new accounting practice only to criticize you, hit you, or take away your corner office with the city view when you make a predictable mistake. You'd want honest feedback, more information on the skill you're trying to acquire or, better yet, some helpful nonverbal reminders or a demonstration of how it should be done.

Infraction-based responses are those actions you'll take related to the skill to be learned or the fence to be accepted. Handing your son the mini-vacuum to pick up the crumbs he dropped during dinner is a better suited action to tell-me, show-me discipline than taking away his television privileges. And remember to always start with small actions when delivering your messages. Big actions are seen by your child as an overreaction. If I'm ten dollars short at the grocery store, I might be asked to leave the groceries until I can return with the ten dollars. I'm not likely to be asked to offer my firstborn as collateral.

Timely responses occur at the time of the behavior you're trying to modify. This is why I don't advocate imposing consequences or punishments at home for challenging behavior at school. Or taking away privileges that don't connect with the behavior in any meaningful way. Your child learns nothing about how to behave differently if your responses are overly negative or are too far removed from behavior you object to. If you're not present when fence-pushing behavior occurs, you can certainly use the situation as an opportunity to be proactive regarding future behavior but you can't do much to undo behavior that happened hours or days ago. Remember, if it happens once it's once; if it happens again it's a theme. Thematic behavior requires a proactive plan for skill building aimed at giving your child positive options for the next time she faces a similar predictable challenge.

Effective responses are those responses that change behavior. There's only one way to discover whether a response is effective or not: trial and error. You'll try a small action to see if it works. If it does, then you have a solution. If it doesn't work, you'll need to try another small action until you find the one that impacts behavior.

Willie is nine and loves to eat. He eats fast and he eats loud. His brothers and sisters are starting to complain about sitting near Willie at mealtime. Willie needs new eating skills. Assume Willie has been told in advance what he can and can't do at dinner, and that an infraction will mean his food will be removed. And assuming he's been given the chance to practice, now his mother can use the RITE response. The RITE response is used to show him the fence is real, the expectation not negotiable. When Willie sees the tell-me discipline matching the show-me discipline, the skills for eating with appropriate manners will go in the bag.

During the next meal, Willie's mother uses a nonverbal reminder that the expectation is not negotiable. She starts by handing him a napkin, then later gestures with her own napkin that it's time to wipe his mouth. She might need to tap his plate or the table as an additional reminder. If Willie is able to eat as he's been taught and as he's practiced, the skills are in the bag, lesson learned. If he's unable to do so, the right response is to follow the gestures and small actions with the removal of his plate—without talking.

Remember, Willie has been prepared for this possibility. In this case, taking away the plate relates to the skills to be learned; it's the right response to the mealtime expectations. This isn't a *take-away* pulled out of nowhere meant to punish, and it isn't a verbal threat or an overreaction. If the expectation is to eat with appropriate manners in order to eat with the family, the right response is to nonverbally remind Willie and then remove the food. What if Willie suddenly says he forgot and he'll adjust his behavior? Then Willie should stay and eat; everyone deserves to start again. After all, if Willie is now using his table manners, your RITE response taught Willie the right response: Eat using appropriate manners.

So, no more "consequences," just the RITE response. Perhaps you see this as only a semantic difference. I see it as a necessary reframing in a world eager to push you into reactive ways of parenting. It might sound simple but at times it's not so easy. Are you ready to see if you can distinguish between the sometimes dramatic and sometimes subtle differences between punishment and skill-building? I'll wager it's easier to see the difference here than it might be in situations involving your child. But like your child, you'll benefit from practice.

Master of Disguise

When you build fences in advance, telling your child what is negotiable and what is not, it's easier to use small actions and nonverbal means of delivering your message during conflict. It's easier to use the RITE response. Do you find you talk a lot when you're in conflict with your child, giving her the message that nonnegotiable behavior is really quite negotiable? Without fences built ahead of potentially difficult situations, the likelihood you'll tend to step in with punishment rather than skill-building is high. Here are some situations you might encounter. See how well you do recognizing the difference between actions that build skill and those that punish.

Skill-building or punishment?

1. A teenager misses her curfew for the third time . . . You ground her for a week.

   Skill-Building   Punishment

2. Two children are fighting over crayons . . . You intervene by giving each child five crayons.

   Skill-Building   Punishment

3. A child reaches up to the counter for a brownie . . . Without talking, you slap his hand.

   Skill-Building   Punishment

4. A creative child draws pictures with his finger on the frosty window panes . . . You hand him a paper towel and window cleaner.

   Skill-Building   Punishment

5. A child repeatedly gets out of bed . . . You tell him if he gets out again you'll take his teddy bear.

   Skill-Building   Punishment

6. Two children are playing loudly while you're on the telephone . . . You snap your fingers once and put a finger to your lips.

   Skill-Building   Punishment

7. A child feeds his dinner to the dog . . . You remove him to the den and tell him to sit there and think

about what he's done; he can't come
back until you say so.

8. During homework, an easily   **Skill-Building   Punishment**
   distracted child repeatedly clicks
   her pen . . . First you cover her hand,
   when it continues, you trade her a
   pencil.

9. A child is having difficulty sharing   **Skill-Building   Punishment**
   her beach toys . . . You tell her if she
   grabs a toy one more time, you'll
   take her home.

10. An active boy often jumps down   **Skill-Building   Punishment**
    stairs from the middle of the
    staircase . . . You have him go back
    up and come down one stair at a time.

How well do you think you did? By now, some examples of
skill-building or punishment are obvious to you while others may
appear more subtle. Here's what each example in the exercise is
teaching.

1. Punishment. Grounding is a technique that removes the child
   but does nothing to teach new skills for accepting fences.
   Counterproductive to good communication, this technique sets
   up a hostile relationship between parent and adolescent. Instead, wait until emotions cool down and build a better fence
   for the next outing.

2. Skill-building. The small action of intervening—giving each
   child a few crayons—delivers the message: Color without arguing. What do you do if the children suddenly believe they can

share? Let them share. Your RITE response taught the right response, to color without arguing.

3. Punishment. Though a clear message was delivered here, hitting a child is reactive, disrespectful, and hurtful. The way this message was delivered actually encourages two types of negative behavior: retaliation behavior, which is behavior a child uses to get back at someone, and defiant behavior, which is behavior aimed at knowingly pushing fences especially when no one is looking. Instead, move the brownies or better yet, don't put yummy chocolate in front of a child unless you'll allow him to eat it.

4. Skill-building. This situation illustrates behavior that is neither right nor wrong, good nor bad; it's simply behavior in need of the RITE response. Through respectful action that fits the situation, the child learns to be cooperative and responsible.

5. Punishment. A threat of a *take-away* neither uncovers the why behind the child's behavior—why is he getting out of bed?—nor does it teach the child to behave differently in the future. Instead, talk about the bedtime routine during the day including his can-dos for getting in bed and staying there. Come bedtime, walk your child back to bed, without talking. Do this as many times as it takes for him to get the message: It's bedtime.

6. Skill-building. Nonverbal gestures communicate as effectively, if not more so, than words. If the children repeatedly have difficulty during phone time, the behavior is thematic and needs a proactive plan for additional skill-building to be taught before the next phone call. And don't forget to practice.

7. Punishment. The use of a time-out when a child engages in developmentally expected, predictable, and preventable behav-

ior is demeaning and unfair. A proactive plan for mealtime, one that includes can-dos and is practiced in advance, will guarantee better behavior for everyone. And don't forget your prevention options—does the dog really have to sit under the table during dinner?

8. Skill-building. Sequential small actions can be taken if the first action doesn't meet with success. Trial and error is the method of choice for finding the actions that impact behavior.

9. Punishment. Going big, by imposing an action disproportionate to and aimed at taking the child out of the game, ensures she'll never learn how to share her toys at the beach. Without the combination of a proactive plan and the RITE response, the next time the child finds herself in this situation, behavior is likely to look exactly the same. Instead, combine tell-me and show-me discipline aimed at teaching the child exactly how sand toys are shared. And then sit near her to guide the sharing.

10. Skill-building. This is an example of the overcorrection technique, which is simply going back and trying something again the way it's been taught proactively. This technique should be used with a light attitude since you're not looking to engage in a power struggle over reclimbing the stairs.

When you're unclear about whether an action you'd like to take is punishment or skill-building, ask yourself whether or not it's the RITE response. Is your response to behavior respectful, based on the infraction, timely, and likely to be effective? Remember, punishment is negative and leads to more punishment while skill-building leads to more skills. With more skills in the bag, your child's overall behavior is more effective. In short, with skill-building, behavior gets better.

Get in the Same Boat

Whether you're learning to ride a bike, drive a car, or sail a boat, everyone benefits from repeated efforts at gaining solid skills. Practice. Maybe you have a child who learns things very quickly and with renewed efforts on your part—with more tell-me, show-me discipline—her bag will be overflowing with new skills in no time. But for many of you, your child's learning will be slower and will require more repetition, more consistency, and more patience on your part.

You've taken the first quiz and examined your parenting style, both your strengths and the areas you'll need to strengthen. You've taken the second quiz aimed at helping you understand how your child's style affects behavioral learning. If you've found your child's style to be agreeable when it comes to accepting fences or you've found your child only has difficulty accepting fences in certain situations, skill-building will be relatively easy. But for the child with the dynamic style, skill-building will be more complex. If your child is hard-wired to push fences more than others, it's essential for you to learn how to work toward your child's temperament, not against it. If your child has a number of strong elements of temperament, you know he's more likely to push fences. So, the next chapter is for you.

10. Parenting Toward Temperament

Alan Alexander adored being a father to his son, Christopher. A writer by trade, he spent his evenings making up stories intended to delight and entertain Christopher. Using Christopher's own toys as characters, stuffed animals became real, enjoying fictional adventures in the very real forest nearby. Alan Alexander was A. A. Milne and his son was Christopher Robin Milne, the central character in the treasured children's stories *Winnie-the-Pooh* and *The House at Pooh Corner*.

Milne gave each animal in his son's stories well-defined qualities, creating one-of-a-kind depictions of animals that could easily have been real children. These much-loved stories remain childhood favorites because every child can connect with at least one of its memorable well-drawn characters. Is your favorite the effervescent Tigger or is it Rabbit, whose relentless obsession to plant a garden keeps him persevering? Maybe you relate better to the easily excited but equally fearful Piglet or have a special place in your heart for the kind and generous lead character himself, Pooh.

Milne, whether inadvertently or intentionally, used the nine elements of temperament to flesh out his unforgettable cast of characters. Each one has positive qualities and brings an unparalleled perspective to the situations the group encounters. Yet each character also strives to overcome personality traits that bring conflict to the Hundred-Acre Wood.

Without each character's individual style of learning and playing, the stories wouldn't have the same charm. Your child has a distinctive style, too, one that is at times equal parts asset and burden.

If your child is kind and thoughtful to his autistic brother, his sensitivity is a major strength for behaving well and making good social decisions. Yet, the same high degree of sensitivity that brings kindness to his relationship with his brother may make it hard for him to shake off the unkind remark of a friend. Every child's strongest elements of temperament have a positive side and a side that presents behavioral challenges. Your role as parent is to celebrate your child's strengths while identifying those aspects of temperament still in need of additional skill-building.

For Better or Worse

If you believe that you've got the power to make your child's behavior better, then you must admit you've also got the power to make behavior worse. Though I'm sure it's the furthest thing from your mind to ever make behavior more challenging, there are some parenting techniques that when paired with certain temperaments make behavior worse. Much worse.

If you have a persistent child, one so adept in his ability to negotiate he could sell you swampland in Florida, talking during conflict will be your undoing. When you talk too much about what's not negotiable, your child sees the discussion still open to debate, dialogue, and discussion. Since your persistent child will likely be insistent he's got the right idea or a better way to do something, if you pick up your end of the rope in a power struggle, so will he. Thing is, he'll never drop his end if you're still talking.

The child hard-wired to be overly sensitive, passionate, and dramatic about her feelings isn't likely to control expressions of emotions any better if her parent reacts to behavior by yelling, screaming, or crying. Matching your intense behavior to your child's teaches her this is how big

> *If you have a persistent child, one so adept in his ability to negotiate he could sell you swampland in Florida, talking during conflict will be your undoing. When you talk too much about what's not negotiable, your child sees the discussion still open to debate, dialogue, and discussion.*

feelings such as joy, sorrow, frustration, anger, and disappointment are managed in her family.

Simply telling the child who struggles with issues of mood to snap out of it, or telling the child who's more easily distracted to get it together will only serve to add to your child's frustration and increase feelings of inadequacy. After all, if your child could look on the bright side or focus his attention on important tasks, he would. If your child knew how to behave in ways that made life easier—if those skills were already in the bag—she would use them.

You can't simply run the active child out. You can't simply ask the inflexible child to go with the flow. You can't simply persuade the introvert to be the life of the party. What you can do is teach your child the skills he needs to channel his activity productively, to compromise on the way situations will be handled, and to socialize in new yet still comfortable ways.

To add skills to your dynamic child's bag, you must learn to work with your child's temperament, not against it. In the following pages, I'll outline proactive skill-building techniques aimed at building solid fences for specific temperaments.

Decisions Made in Lower Court

Pete is a ten-year-old who enjoys spending time with his dad doing Saturday errands. Last weekend after errands were done, Pete convinced his dad to stop into a video game store, just to browse. After Pete begs and pleads to get a new game, his dad gives in and Pete walks out of the store, new game in hand. All week, Pete and his friends enjoyed playing it. The levels were mastered and secrets of the game revealed, so Pete got it in his mind this weekend that he'd like another new game. "Dad, I can't wait until we stop at the game store. I really want the next game in the series."

"Wait a minute. You're not getting another new video game. I just got you one last weekend."

"Dad, I'll pay for it with my own money. Please?"

Later that afternoon, after making numerous arguments that sounded like expert testimony, Pete steered his dad into the game store. With his own wallet in hand, and his relentless pursuit of the game in full swing, Pete got a new video game.

Give an inch, take a mile. Do something once and you can expect your persistent Pete to want to do it over and over again. Precedents are defined in legal circles as the rules by which other similar situations must be compared. Precedent-setting parenting, a decision you make once, sets the stage for how your child will think future situations will be handled. The persistent child sees tell-me, show-me connections faster than you can make them. In light of this, you must be very careful which precedents you set and what tell-me, show-me discipline you put together.

When Pete's dad bought the first video game, he had a perfect opportunity to head off more persistence later. "Pete, I'd like to buy you this video game today but only if you can agree it's going to be the only one we buy this month. Repeat after me, This is the game for this month."

By creating fences in advance and building in personal account-ability, you've set the stage for limited talking in the nonnegotiable situation later. And remember, you don't want to pick up the rope of a power struggle especially once you've deemed something non-negotiable.

The persistent child benefits from lots of solid fences with the freedom found in the backyard made very clear. Tell-me, show-me connections made consistently and with certainty will be critical to your child's ability to let go and move on once you've made expec-tations clear. Give your bright and independent child control over age-appropriate decisions. Put his leadership qualities to work for your family. Ask him to plan how weekend chores will get done or have him research your top two family vacation destinations.

When the persistent child is mobilized into productive action, look out: He's a force to be admired. But remember, the deter-mined child pushes fences more when fences are unclear or when fences are too harsh. As soon as you realize you're negotiating away your authority, stop talking about that which is not negotiable. Then be proactive for the next situation, offering appropriate free-doms for your persistent child right in his own backyard.

Mountains High and Valleys Low

Passionate and able to feel things deeply, Izzy is described by her parents as a child with high highs and low lows. One minute she's happy, laughing and thinking life is grand. And the next, doors are slamming, feet are stomping, and she's yelling so loud her parents wonder what the neighbors must be thinking.

Izzy's parents admit they sometimes make her intense behavior worse by trying to talk her out of being upset. When they touch her or try to move her to a different location she claims they're hurting her. Her behavior becomes so extreme at times, they worry for her safety. The number-one strategy they use now to manage Izzy's behavior is trying to tiptoe around her so she won't blow up. But they haven't had much success with this tactic.

The intense child is hard-wired to feel things deeply and she has a strong need to get feelings conveyed in dramatic ways so others understand just how big these feelings are. If you have an intense child, you may be very tempted to ask what to do when your child blows up or melts down. Keeping your child safe from harm is first and foremost when intense behavior surfaces. But the real key to parenting the intense child is not waiting until behavior is out of control and asking "what do I do when . . ." Instead, the goal is to build skills for managing intensity in predictable situations. And this must be done in advance, when your child is calm.

In the story *Goldilocks and the Three Bears*, Goldilocks happens upon a cottage and when she enters it, she finds everything comes in extremes. The porridge is too hot, too cold, and just right. The chairs are too hard, too soft, and just right. Using the story of the three bears, you can help your child understand that she often expresses her feelings in ways that are too big and that you're going to help her learn to expresses her feelings "just right."

After reading or telling the story, use typical situations she faces every day to discuss what "just right" responses look like. Discuss with your child what she can do when overwhelming feelings start to surface. Can she take a deep breath, go running, write in a journal, listen to music, use some clay, take a bath, or ask you to hold her? Use any of these strategies as well as any others you think will help your intense child get feelings under control first, so she can move on to solve problems later.

Make a list of these "can-dos." Then practice with your child how to use these strategies to get her expressions of behavior "just right." Tell her how you'll intervene when there's a high-high or a low-low. Remind her you won't talk in the conflict situations she faces if the way she expresses herself is "too big." Tell her you'll stay present and perhaps role-model taking a deep breath or point to the list of can-dos you've made together or hand her a journal. But you won't talk. When you gesture and use small actions during conflict rather than talk, you help diffuse intensity. Talking at or to a child who is "too big" is like adding a log to a smoldering fire. You'll only make the behavior worse.

Skill-building for the intense child begins with predicting, preparing, and practicing. If or when your child becomes intense, you intervene without talking because you don't want to make the explosive behavior negotiable. Once your child has cooled down, let her know the good things she did to manage her big feelings and let her know what she can do differently the next time. What you teach with this combination of tell-me, show-me discipline is how your child can take accountability for her own behavior and still get problems solved.

Intensity skill-building is a process and will take time. Though your child's behavior may sometimes seem extreme, I assure you she would rather be able to express her feelings more effectively. She needs you to teach her how, first by being proactive and then by staying close and remaining firm.

If, in the past, you've either wavered or been reactive in dealing with your child's intensity, she will assume the more dramatic she gets, the more likely you'll give in to her outbursts. In light of this, once you put a skill-building plan in place, her intensity may at first appear to get worse. Behavior that gets bigger before it gets better is called an extinction burst. Don't underestimate the power of preparation and practice; remember, vicarious learning counts. If connections are made consistently, your intense child will gain skill for managing big feelings. She'll begin to understand what "just right" looks and feels like, being better able to find "just right" with each situation she faces all on her own. Then life will indeed be grand for you, your child, and for the entire family. Maybe even the neighbors.

Half-empty Glasses

Eeyore, the gloomy donkey in the *Winnie-the-Pooh* stories struggles with issues of mood. When faced with a new challenge, can't you just imagine him saying, "Oh no, this isn't going to go well."

If your child struggles with moodiness, she may be described by you or others as anxious, worried, negative, pessimistic, or fearful. In short, she sees the glass half-empty instead of half-full. Your child's view of the world is hard-wired, and though you can't change the hard-wiring, you can change the skills she has to contend with it.

From a very early age, seven-year-old Mamie has approached the world with worry. "Will I be able to do this?" "I don't think I can do that." "I'm afraid." Mamie loses sleep every night for one reason or another. Lately, she's been focused on whether or not the fire alarm in her room is working.

For the last week, Mamie has been reluctant to go to bed. And once there, she keeps calling her mother in to check the fire alarm. Her mother continues to reassure her everything is fine. She double checks it and repeatedly tells Mamie she wouldn't leave her in the room if she didn't think it was working. But yesterday, Mamie's mother got so tired of checking the alarm and so frustrated she wasn't able to convince her daughter things were fine, she let Mamie sleep in her room on the floor.

If you have a child like Mamie, your natural response is to talk her through concerns and fears. *You'll be fine. You've got nothing to worry about.* If dispelling fears and disregarding concerns were as easy as convincing your child all's well, you wouldn't become increasingly frustrated like Mamie's mother. Your child would simply accept your reassurance and everything would truly be fine.

In proactive parenting, action comes first. Feelings will follow. Though it might seem counterintuitive, talking about worry reinforces worry. The more you talk when your child is deeply anxious or fearful, the more you reinforce to your child she really has something to be concerned about. After

> *The more you talk when your child is deeply anxious or fearful, the more you reinforce to your child she really has something to be concerned about.*

all, why would you spend so much time trying to convince her she doesn't have anything to worry about, if she doesn't have anything to worry about?

I'm not saying you can't ever talk about worries, fears, or concerns. You can and you should, but once again you've got to know when to talk and when to act. The best time to talk about a child's fear is before the fear arises—if you can predict, you can prevent. Skill-building for the child who struggles with issues of mood is done when the child isn't fearful.

Mamie's mother turned things around when she used a powerful technique with her child; it's called the projecting technique. During the day, she asked Mamie what she thought the worst-case scenario was, given her fear about the fire alarm. Mamie said she was afraid there'd be a fire and her alarm wouldn't go off. Then she feared that even if hers did go off, she'd sleep through it.

When you use the projecting technique before anxiety takes hold, you help your child talk out irrational fears or inaccurate worries. Once your child says out loud what she's afraid of, either she realizes it's not that worrisome or it gives you a chance to reassure the fear isn't justified using action, not more talking. Once Mamie expressed her fear, her mother showed her the fire alarms all had fresh batteries. She pointed out the red light on each alarm indicating they were working. She even tested an alarm, showing Mamie how hard it would be to sleep through the noise it makes. She was also able to prepare Mamie for bedtime the next night, telling her she wouldn't be talking about this at bedtime anymore. If she had any other concerns, now was the time to voice them.

The anxious child may worry about any number of things and clearly needs more skills than others do to handle her fears. She needs coping strategies. Once again, you'll want to help your child identify the action-oriented can-dos she might use when she worries. Can she take a special belonging such as a cherished bracelet or stuffed animal to school? Can she draw, write in a journal, pray the rosary, play an instrument, or exercise to channel the worry productively? All of these strategies move feelings to action, empowering your child to become familiar with her feelings and then do something about them. She learns to rely on herself, not you, in dealing with negative feelings.

Often the use of these proactive techniques eliminates anxiety or, at the very least, reduces it. Always be prepared to follow through with actions, not talking, if and when your child becomes anxious. Tell your child in advance, you'll only talk about her concerns once she's taken a can-do action first. What you teach with this combination of tell-me, show-me discipline is that all feelings are acceptable; it's what you do about them that counts.

Hocus-pocus Focus

If you could wave a magic wand to help your child get focused, I'm certain you would. Life is easier for the child who can listen intently, complete every project, and remember everything he learns. But learning how to pay attention when you're hard-wired to be more distracted just isn't that easy. It will take more than a magic trick to help your child concentrate on what's important and what's not, as well as how to get necessary tasks accomplished. You'll need to put attention skills in the bag.

Oscar is a fifth-grade boy who loves everything; everything that is, except school. Always socializing, Oscar is everyone's best friend but he's increasingly having difficulty working up to potential at school. Sometimes his work is messy, sometimes incomplete. And his father would tell you homework is a nightmare.

"First he can't find a pencil and paper. Then he gets out his homework planner and nothing's written down. Once I finally get him settled, then he's up to go to the bathroom and I find him playing with the cat. I know he's smart, I don't know why he doesn't want to do well. I'm tired of seeing him choose to do everything except what he's supposed to be doing. He's getting lazier by the day."

Choosing to do poorly. Not wanting to do well. Lazy. I can't tell you how often I hear parents describe the distractible and clearly misunderstood child as lazy. If your child has difficulty prioritizing his work, slowing down, striving for quality work, or remembering what he's studied, he's either too young for the expectations or he's hard-wired to be more distractible. With any skill-building, it's important to tease out whether limited skills relate to age and development or relate to temperament. Either way, your child isn't getting distracted on purpose. If he had the skills to make lists, manage time, follow rules of grammar, remember math formulas, and spell correctly, he would. The child who struggles with being distracted by sights, sounds, and smells is a child who has obstacles in the path of his success.

Imagine you're going on a trip. After you find your keys and collect your bags you get in your car and begin driving. Not long into your journey, you're traveling down a road and suddenly see several bright orange cones in the road. You're an experienced driver, and you know how to get around cones in the road. For the child who is easily distracted, learning is like this road trip. The trouble is, the distractible child sometimes has difficulty beginning the journey; and sometimes when he reaches a cone in the road, he simply doesn't know how to get around it. He's stuck.

The skill-building that's required for Oscar, and your distracted child, must be centered on building external means of being organized and focused. Since he lacks the skills in his bag to set the right pace, to be consistent in his efforts, and to plan ahead, he's got to be taught how these challenges in learning are managed. Timers, schedules, checklists, dry-erase boards, and homework supply drawers are all proactive steps you can take to set your child up to be organized.

Well before homework time, you and your child should decide on the location, time, and duration of homework. Keep your child close until he proves successful with the new plan, as the further away from you he gets, the more likely he'll get caught up in other more interesting pursuits. Order his homework from hardest to easiest. By the time your child is getting more tired and more distracted, all he has left are the easier assignments. Keep in mind, your child may do better with homework in the morning rather than in the afternoon and be aware, few who are easily distracted do well completing homework at night. Help your child break big projects into smaller, more manageable parts, to be spread out over a longer period of time. Use the three-night rule for tests. On nights one and two study, read, and be quizzed. On night three, review and go to bed early.

Does this sound good in theory but you're worried about putting it into practice? Your child may engage in characteristic avoidance behavior. The work is hard, so he'll try to get out of it. "I need to sharpen my pencil." "Can I have another snack?" These behaviors are common and should be extinguished. But how?

You and your child should design and discuss the homework plan in advance; be proactive. But you'll also have to share with your child the nonverbal cues and small actions you'll take to get him back on track. Walk him back to the homework desk. Tap his paper. Hand him a pencil. Whatever you decide to do to refocus his attention during homework time, don't talk. When you talk to the easily distractible child during a task that requires focus, you are an additional distraction. You're likely to end up in a power struggle, too. To the distractible child, power struggles serve as another way to avoid doing homework.

Oscar's new homework plan included doing homework right after a snack. He'd eat, then do some sit-ups and push-ups to get more alert. Then he'd sit at the kitchen table with his agenda. His dad helped him make a list of things he'd do that day on a small dry-erase board he kept on the table along with a timer. In math for example, Oscar would work for ten minutes. Once his dad checked to see he was on the right track, Oscar would continue. If he was having difficulty, his dad would explain the problems or allow him to move to a different set. But at least Oscar wouldn't have done all the problems incorrectly, only leading to feelings of inadequacy and wanting to give up. Did Dad need to refocus Oscar's attention from time to time? Of course. But over time, he and Oscar learned where to build in the right breaks at the best times. They started to work together. It wasn't an illusion when Oscar's dad started seeing just how much Oscar wanted to be successful and how much he enjoyed doing well. Oscar didn't need a magic potion or special charm; he needed a coach, he needed a teacher. He needed his dad.

Sticks and Stones

Ask any friend or family member to tell you about childhood friendships and you'll hear story after story of big misunderstandings, broken promises, and hurt feelings. Each of us has at least one memory, brought easily into sharp focus, of feeling left out. Maybe you still have these feelings, for some making friends and keeping friends is very hard work, no matter how old you are.

This is especially true for the child hard-wired to dive into friendships, coming on too strong, and for the child who stands back, hoping friendship will find him. In these instances, social skill development is more difficult.

Rita is concerned about five-year-old Seth's ability to make friends. Given the choice, Seth would play alone every day with his animal figures and blocks. He builds detailed zoos and jungles; his imaginative play is fun to watch. While Rita is happy Seth can play well alone, she'd also like him to be able to play well with others his age. Hard-wired to approach new people and new situations with caution, Seth will need more exposure and experience with social situations. Seth needs more effective social skills in his bag.

If your child has brothers and sisters and is social by nature, you don't need to jump on the play-date bandwagon. While having children over for arranged social experiences is certainly fun and fine, the natural experience your child gets at home, in the neighborhood, and at school is sufficient for social skill-building. Unless like Seth, your child could benefit from extra practice developing skills that *a short and structured play date* might offer.

Two days in advance, Rita arranged for a child from Seth's kindergarten class to come over after school to play. Before the child arrived, Rita told Seth he and his friend would play something inside, something outside, have a snack, and then they'd drive the friend home. She gave Seth the freedom to choose what things the boys might play. Rita continued to be proactive when she predicted Seth would have difficulty with sharing, talking, and compromising when his friend was over. And because she was proactive, she was able to prevent certain issues while she prepared Seth for others.

"Seth, you did a great job organizing the zoo toys in your room yesterday. I bet you're really proud of that. When your friend comes over tomorrow, are you going to play downstairs and not risk getting your zoo messed up or should we talk about how to handle it when things get disturbed? If you do choose to play with the zoo, it is likely to get moved or even knocked over. Let's practice what you can say and what you can do."

Rita used two strategies that strongly predict social success: role-playing and scripting. Role-playing is a great way to practice social ins and outs, but so too is the use of scripting. Scripting involves giving your child the actual things he can say in social situations and then letting him practice beforehand. In any new social situation, your child first must think up what to say and then he must say it. If you offer an appropriate script in advance, you've cut the difficulty of the social situation in half.

Rita made the most of her proactive plan for social success when she told Seth what she would do to help him once his friend was over. "Seth, I know you like to play alone. But when your friend is here, you'll need to play with him. If you wander off, I'll walk you back to where your friend is playing. If you aren't talking enough, I'll come over and put my hand on your shoulder to remind you. And when your friend goes home, you can have all the alone time you'd like."

Small actions and nonverbal cueing. When your child is learning social skills, the best time to talk, role-play, and script is before the social situation. The reason you stop talking when your child is in the social situation is because if you do the talking, he doesn't have to. For the child who struggles with social skills, he'll be tempted to rely on you too much when it comes to forming his friendships. Slowly but surely you want to hold your child accountable for doing what it takes to enjoy social success.

Keep in mind, there's a difference between the child who *can* socialize but chooses not to and the child who *can't* socialize and wants to. Social skill development is very effective when you start small, increase exposure and experience little by little, and then expect your child to successfully demonstrate what he's learned in practice.

Promise You'll Never Change

Why is it some people love to travel, can't wait to redecorate their living rooms, or don't mind moving, while others dread each and every one of those experiences? Flexible or inflexible. Adventure seeker or homebody. How do you adapt to change and manage the unexpected?

For the child who adapts slowly or poorly, adjusting to complicated daily routines, shifting schedules, or new school years are just a few life events she'll find unsettling.

Addy is an eight-year-old who's well aware of how much she hates change. She hasn't removed a poster from the wall, a knick-knack from her shelf, or the bedspread on her bed since she originally placed each there. The big news her parents must break to her is that the family is moving across the country. Like Addy's parents, you can probably guess this move will be extremely difficult for Addy. Her hard-wiring, and maybe your child's, too, makes embracing change very challenging unless there's lots of preparation.

Preparation can come in the form of time lines, family meetings, lists of can-dos, and any other way you can think of to move your child's feelings to action. Skill-building will be critical if Addy is to feel control over a situation that will likely make her feel out of control. While she should be given the opportunity to express her reluctance to move, she still must move. The best thing her parents can do is give her hands-on ways of adapting to what's expected of her. Given concrete tasks to accomplish, such as collecting addresses and phone numbers of friends, visiting her new school, and choosing how she'll decorate her new room, Addy can begin to ease herself toward the change instead of trying to withdraw from it.

Whether your child needs to change her shoes, change her mind, or change where she lives, validating your child's feelings of reluctance toward change is important. But once the time to change is upon her, you'll need to guide her

> *Behavioral feedback entails giving your child specific concrete examples of what she's doing well in reaching her goals and leaving her with one thing she can continue to work on or strive for.*

through the process, regardless of the discomfort she'll feel. The single most important strategy to use with the child who adapts slowly is to teach her how to begin getting comfortable with change. If you can predict it, you can prepare her. And don't forget to tell her how she's doing.

Each time your child makes a step toward becoming more flexible, be sure to give her positive feedback. Behavioral feedback entails giving your child specific concrete examples of what she's doing well in reaching her goals and leaving her with one thing she can continue to work on or strive for. Addy's mom gave her daughter behavioral feedback when she said, "Addy, the way you organized your e-mail addresses is going to make it a lot easier to keep in touch with friends. Would you help me with mine?" "I know you aren't ready to start packing your entire room but next week we're going to start with organizing and packing up your desk. I'll help you get started."

Every child needs to hear about the job well done, not just the job *not* done. Give your child the encouragement she needs to keep putting skills in her bag. Because no matter where she lives, she'll be taking the bag with her.

When in Rome

The rhythms of your body, the way you eat, sleep, and even how regularly you go to the bathroom are hard-wired. The element of temperament that dictates your biorhythms is called physical regularity. Does your child have an unpredictable rhythm, making her spontaneous and go with the flow when it comes to activities of daily living? Or does your child need to eat meals on a regular schedule, fall asleep whenever the clock strikes bedtime, and wake up at the same time each morning, even on weekends? I happen to have one of each type of child, so in order to work toward temperament not against it, I'm required to plan life around the child with the more rigid need for schedules.

Florence, also a mother of two, wonders if it's fair. "I feel bad for my nine-year-old, Clarence, because my four-year-old, George, needs so much attention. If I don't feed him, he's cranky. If he doesn't go to bed on time, he's a bear. And when it comes to getting dressed, forget it. He hates tags and socks and coats and boots. I swear he's happiest in summer, when he doesn't have to wear much clothing."

George has predictable though somewhat inflexible physical rhythms, partly attributed to his age and partly due to his temperament. But he struggles with another element of temperament too: physical sensitivity. One child may struggle with emotional sensitivity, another may struggle with how sensitive their body is to things; some struggle with both.

If Florence is going to begin working toward George's temperament, first she'll need to predict the times of day he has the most difficulty and then prevent the inevitable power struggles. If he needs set mealtimes and bedtimes, she should make these times sacred as best she can. Next she'll need to build skills for handling tricky situations like his sensitivity to clothing. She can begin by assessing all of George's clothes to be sure there aren't any with tight collars or sleeves, itchy material, or uncomfortable seams. Proactively she can talk with George about how dressing will go, she can show him where the clothes that feel best given his sensitivities are located, and of course they ought to practice. But once it's time to get dressed—the talking is over. Either he gets dressed or she dresses him; wearing clothes isn't negotiable.

Like Florence, you might worry that you're short-changing one child in favor of skill-building with another. But you needn't worry, because when the child who requires more attention and more skill-building behaves well, everyone benefits. Certainly, you'll have to juggle one child's need for routine, structure, and skill-building with your other child's need to go with the flow and be spontaneous, but that's been at the heart of parenting for generations.

Stress Rehearsal

For the child who is more—more persistent, intense, sensitive, moody, resistant to change, or distractible—you need more strategies for parenting. Whatever combination of strategies you use to skill-build, more will be needed and more will be better. Highlight can-dos. Encourage journaling. Project what the worst-case scenario is likely to look and feel like. Role-play. Use children's books to encourage dialogue. Script social situations. Provide physical and creative outlets. All of these techniques build skill. Building skill fills the bag with new ways of behaving, giving your child more effective ways of relating to others.

Once you've got more strategies, you're ready to teach. Now that you're ready, it's time to be sure your child is ready. It's easier to learn new things when you're relaxed and ready to learn. It's harder to learn new things when you are trying to learn too many new things at once, you don't feel well, or you've got family issues on your mind. The same is true for your child. When stress goes up, behavioral learning slows down and sometimes even goes backward. Learning that goes backward is called regression.

Three-year-old Matteo has been successful using the toilet independently for two months. He's been going to a new preschool, but his attendance over the past month has been sporadic because of recurrent ear infections. His mother has been traveling more than usual for her job and the family dog is ill. This week, Matteo hasn't been making it to the bathroom in time and has asked his dad if he can go back to diapers. Matteo has regressed in his ability to use the toilet independently.

Under stress, which can be described as any positive or negative experience that must be managed with extra energy, the last skill in the bag is often the hardest skill to locate. Matteo doesn't lose the skill he's already acquired; he's simply misplaced where he put it in his bag. He's preoccupied with everything else he must manage physically and emotionally, so the toilet training has been pushed aside in favor of managing the other aspects of his little life. Once his stress is under control or eliminated, he'll go right back to using the bathroom independently, provided good fences go up to assist him in remembering what he's already learned.

Mental, emotional, or physical pressure—stress—impacts learning in profound ways. That's why the lifestyle choices you make for your child are worthy of an entire section of this book, Part IV. The final quiz is coming up, where you'll find out if your lifestyle is adult-driven or child-friendly.

part four
Lifestyle

11. The Adult-Driven Family

The beach at dusk is a child's wonderland. You don't have to watch where you're stepping, dodging beach blankets and coolers. It's okay to have sand in your shoes or better yet, go barefoot. You're allowed to climb the lifeguard chair and you can run as fast and as far as you want. Sometimes you even get to sit in the sand while your ice cream trickles from your cone down your fingers and onto your pants.

Other families have packed up and are gone for the day but you don't have to go yet. You can play Frisbee with your dad, loving it when he dives to catch your erratic throw. Or you can walk the beach with your mother, thinking how pretty she looks in her kerchief and capri pants, finding it hard to believe she doesn't care that your pants are getting wet.

Time. Time to laugh. Time to play. The summer nights I spent as a child with my parents and siblings are the fondest memories of my childhood. I remember very little about my everyday life as a child. Very few birthday or Christmas gifts stand out in my mind. I don't recall the details of a single Girl Scout meeting or tennis lesson. I can't recollect whether I had help with my homework, if my mother was on the PTA board, or the number of back-to-school skirts she bought me. What I do remember with incredible clarity—and cherish still—are the simple pleasures I found on a Cape Cod beach, when what I was allowed to be was a child.

The Time of Your Life

Childhood officially begins the day your child is born. But when does it officially end? Some say it ends when your child starts school. Some claim it ends when your child finally realizes life isn't fair. But with confidence I can tell you this: True childhood is getting shorter and shorter with each passing day, each passing year. In fact, some claim childhood is disappearing altogether.

What does it mean to be a child today? Play dates are orchestrated. Tests are standardized and timed. Shoes have wheels, toddlers have miniature grocery carts, and teenagers have their own cars. There are structured activities for babies, spa treatments for preschoolers, and entrance exams for kindergarteners. There's less recess and shorter lunch breaks, more homework and scheduled activities. Less time to play. Less family time.

Every child who's distractible and every student who feels stressed does not have a diagnosis like ADD or depression. There's another more likely explanation: the adult-driven lifestyle.

The pace of life is swift, getting faster and faster every day. It's not enough to do more; you've got to have more and do better than anyone else at whatever you take on. But is anyone really getting ahead? It's like the expression "The faster I go the behinder I get."

Maybe you have a child who is successful managing the complexities of daily life. Perhaps she has so many skills already in her bag that a fast-paced life suits her. The statistics on childhood behavioral diagnoses such as autism spectrum disorders, attention deficit hyperactivity disorder, depression, bipolar disorder, sensory integration dysfunction, and the list goes on, tell another story. But every child who's distractible and every student who feels stressed does not have a diagnosis like ADD or depression. There's another more likely explanation: the adult-driven lifestyle.

June is increasingly concerned about the reports she's getting from her daughter Glory's preschool teachers. Teachers say after drop-off she's clingy, edgy with her friends, and can't seem to find a morning activity that interests her. As the day progresses, Glory gets silly or agitated and she can't settle in to the afternoon routine. According to June, Glory is hard to put to bed at night and equally hard to get up in the morning.

Some might be tempted to cast a wide net to explain Glory's behavior and want to evaluate her for a diagnosis of attention deficit hyperactivity disorder. But casting a small net first is best. When June and I looked at a typical day for her four-year-old, it became clear there were some lifestyle factors that, if modified, could give June a truer picture of Glory's behavior.

June began by changing Glory's bedtime from 11 P.M. to 7:30 P.M. Instead of three meals spaced between five and six hours apart, Glory ate six small meals of quality food over the course of her day. And her five after-preschool activities were reduced to one dance class on the weekend. In one week of the new lifestyle, Glory's behavior at school dramatically improved. The teachers and June agreed, Glory was doing just fine.

Was it hard for June to rearrange her daily routine at home and her schedule at work in order to give Glory's new routine a try? It was, and I respect the sacrifice June made in order to make these lifestyle changes. Making change is never easy at first. But when Glory's behavior noticeably improved without behavioral testing, doctor's visits, and trips to the pharmacy for medication, June saved precious time. Time she could spend with Glory. Time she could use to create a child-friendly lifestyle for her daughter. Most important, her daughter's behavior had a more accurate explanation.

What You See Is What You Get

Some parents naturally challenge this cast-a-small-net-first approach, claiming there are certainly plenty of accurate diagnoses made by qualified well-trained professionals every day. I don't disagree. But I'm certain there are many more toddlers, preschoolers, school-age children, and adolescents whose behavior looks diagnostic or who get labeled with a diagnosis when it's their lifestyle that is the real culprit. An adult lifestyle imposed on a child who struggles with learning or who has strong elements of temperament, or who lacks the right skills in the bag may very well create behavior that resembles a diagnosis like the ones listed above.

Laura, mother of eight-year-old Eddie and twelve-year-old Theo, feels like she's in a constant struggle to meet the needs of her boys. "My eight-year-old comes home from school and sits right down to do his homework. He goes to bed when he's supposed to. And on the weekends, you'd hardly even know he's there; he doesn't give me a bit of trouble. But Theo is exhausting; it must be all those hormones. I don't get home from work until seven and he hasn't even started his homework. Then he fights me every night about going to bed. Once I finally get him into his room, that's when he decides to tell me all the things he's got on his mind.

And on the weekends when all I want to do is catch up on chores or read the paper, all I hear from the neighborhood kids is, 'Theo, cut it out.' 'Theo, stop it.' Why can't he just behave?"

There are a number of reasons why you might impose an adult lifestyle on your child. Perhaps you have a child who's easygoing like Eddie. You might be tempted to compare his bag of skills to your other child, a child more like Theo. It's easy to assume if one child—in this case, the younger child—can meet your expectations, so should your other child.

In Laura's situation, her Monday through Friday late-work schedule coupled with her need for downtime on the weekend may fit with Eddie's needs for parenting. But her lifestyle has a significant effect on Theo's need for additional skill-building. Theo needs more help with homework, more effective means of expressing his feelings, and new skills for socializing with friends. And none of this has anything to do with hormones! Comparing Theo's bag to Eddie's bag won't help Laura parent more proactively. It won't help Theo gain new and necessary skills. And I'll bet it does little to make either brother more accepting of the other.

Each child's bag has different strengths and different skills that need refinement. And some skills aren't yet in the bag. When you try to measure one child's success by making comparisons with another child, one will always fall short. Remember, there are no right or wrong bags, just different bags.

> When I hear parents like Laura say, "Why do I have to say the same things over and over again, he knows what I expect him to do," or, "I don't have time for this, why can't he just behave?" I hear a parent who's stressed. And if you're stressed, you can count on your child being stressed, too.

When I hear parents like Laura say, "Why do I have to say the same things over and over again, he knows what I expect him to do," or, "I don't have time for this, why can't he just behave?" I hear a parent who's stressed. And if you're stressed, you can count on your child to be stressed, too.

You've got a bag full of life skills, learned by repeated experience, exposure, and maybe even active skill-building, for how to manage time and meet the expectations others have of you. And yet you may still feel your lifestyle is stressful. Now try to imagine how your child, whose bag is only beginning to contain the life skills he needs to be successful, feels when faced with the same high expectations and pressure to do more, have more, and behave well. When you try to determine what's in your child's bag by making comparisons to your adult bag, he'll always fall short in one way or another.

There's No Time Like the Present

Today, more parents work outside the home. Technology has made a huge impact on the ability to keep families entertained and connected. Every day, your child is exposed to some new product that will make life easier or at least make him seem cooler to his friends. Life is different these days.

In many ways, life is better. Certain childhood diseases have been all but eradicated. Research on childhood behavioral conditions and effective treatments help parents and professionals manage behavioral disorders in ways not available until now. New information about our bodies and our minds guide child care, parenting, health care, and educational practices. And who doesn't love the Internet? But in other ways, life is tougher.

The pace of life, the pressure on you, and the temptations your child faces are over the top. Perhaps what's expected of you as a parent in this new age is beyond your current skill level. Because without a doubt, what's expected of your child is beyond his skill level. Media influence is high just when adult supervision is low. The very technology capable of keeping you connected has members of your family disconnected while sitting in the very same room. One person's talking on a cell phone while another is chatting online.

While the norms of yesterday weren't perfect, today's norms pose new discipline challenges for you and your child. The world has definitely changed, but what your child is capable of and what she needs to grow up to be a person of character has not. Just because your lifestyle is busy doesn't change what your child requires to learn skills and behave well.

Shaping character—getting skills in the bag—takes time. No matter what cultural period a child grows up in, someone needs to monitor sleep and nutrition and intervene over friendship issues and sibling squabbles. Someone needs to spend time building fences and offering age-appropriate freedom within the backyard. Every child, in every generation, needs a parent.

How much time do you spend with your child on an average day? Take yesterday, for example. Think about what you talked about, what you did together. Don't count driving to and from activities or watching his game, unless you were talking—not lecturing or nagging—and skill-building. You can count the time you spent *acting*—

> *The pace of life, the pressure on you, and the temptations your child faces are over the top. Perhaps what's expected of you as a parent in this new age is beyond your current skill level. Because without a doubt, what's expected of your child is beyond his skill level.*

maybe you spent your time being certain your child couldn't negotiate that which is not negotiable.

You won't be able to shape character or change what's in the bag if you're not spending time with your child. And that means once you've gotten to know your child's bag, you've got to take the time to fill it with the skills he needs to be successful. Your investment of time today shapes his character for tomorrow.

It's the best of times and the worst of times to be a parent and to be a child. There are wonderful opportunities and frightening possibilities available to your child. Your child will be exposed to amazing things and shocking things. Every generation has faced both good times and bad influences. It's easy to say the past was a simpler time, a better time. But you've got to live in the here and now; your child is growing up in today's world. So embrace the best of it and reject the worst of it.

While the norms of yesterday weren't perfect, today's norms pose new discipline challenges for you and your child. The world has definitely changed, but what your child is capable of and what she needs to grow up to be a person of character has not.

What Do You Expect?

My three-year-old won't sleep in his bed. My five-year-old won't play with anything but computer games. My seven-year-old won't eat his vegetables. My ten-year-old won't wear her coat.

Today's child has a lot of power: Power that belongs to you. You've got the power to shape your family life, but only if you believe you do.

Dana loves to sleep. As the busy mother of one-year-old twins, sleep is always on her mind. Ruby and Jo share a room. They take scheduled naps and have a set bedtime. The fences built for healthy sleep habits are very important to Dana. "My sister and my friends are constantly pushing me to lighten up on the children's sleep schedule. But I'm committed to sticking with what works for me and what works for my babies. I can't take care of them when I'm exhausted. And they have so much more trouble during the day if I mess with their naptime or bedtime. There'll be plenty of time to socialize when they're older."

Dana is unwavering in her commitment to the fences she's built around sleep. Every parent has strong beliefs about some aspects of child rearing. Perhaps for you, like Dana, it's sleep. Or maybe you're dedicated to providing healthy nutrition, or you feel strongly about the amount of television your child watches. Whatever your strong positions are, when you're committed to a particular nonnegotiable issue, somehow you make your fences very clear and very real for your child. Commitment is the key to solid fence building.

Unfortunately, those around you will test your resolve to stick to the fences you believe in, the ones you know work for you and your child. Whether you're trying to protect your child's sleep schedule, curb the number of sports your child plays, or limit the number of advanced placement classes your child takes, the pressure will be turned on and intensified. But you don't have to get pulled into the Negotiation Generation even though this kind of pressure is hard to withstand.

Your child will be pushed to read, write, and calculate earlier than at any other time in history. Academic expectations keep soaring, but child development hasn't changed. Certainly you can enhance development but you can't change general readiness to learn. Let's say you wanted to teach your two-year-old to memorize the capitals of all the states. He's likely to have difficulty trying to meet your expectation. But perhaps you're successful with this high standard or expectation; does that mean other parents should raise the bar and expect their child to memorize capitals at age two? Certainly not. Yet raising standards for all by comparing everyone's bag to a few is happening in every school, and on every playground. And this disturbing trend may make your child appear to have a behavioral problem when he does not.

Think back to what you were learning in high school; that's what's being taught in middle school right now. What was formerly taught in middle school is now being taught in elementary school. And the trickle-down effect continues. Preschoolers graduate. Toddlers sit at desks. The prevailing educational belief is rush, hurry, push, there's a lot to learn and time is running out. The academic pressure today is enormous and your child may very easily be the one who is left behind.

Social expectations are equally high for your child. With more structured activities and more play dates you'd think every child's bag would be overflowing with social skills. Yet it's becoming more and more common to see a child experience great difficulty figuring out what to do with free time that's unstructured by adults. Does your child freely use her imagination in play and think critically about social problems and their potential solutions? For the young child today, the prevailing thinking is "the more activities the better." Unfortunately, by the time a child reaches high school he's tired of structure and he just wants to hang out, destress, relax. He's burned out from the busy schedule he's been keeping up for years. Offer him a new activity, and you're likely to be met with a "been there, done that," attitude.

A young child should eat and sleep regularly; she should play often and be encouraged to freely use her imagination. She doesn't need structured activity after structured activity. It's your teenager who should be engaged in structured adult supervised programs, clubs, and organizations or have a job. Keeping your older child involved in productive activities and exposed to positive role models will go a long way toward keeping your child safe. In turn, this will increase the chances he'll make good decisions when he's not with you, too.

Oddly enough, while academic and social expectations sky-rocket, behavioral expectations are at an all-time low. Those who waver make excuses for behavior bypassing personal accountability. "He's just a kid." "He didn't mean to." "I'm sure he's sorry." And those who react are kicking kids

> *Oddly enough while academic and social expectations skyrocket, behavioral expectations are at an all-time low.*

out of preschool, sending ten-year-olds to brat camp, and placing fourteen-year-olds in jail, later trying them as adults.

There is a better way. Starting now, you can proactively build a lifestyle that fits your child. Simple *is* better. Simplify.

The Final Test

Once again, remember not to play the blame game. The lifestyle quiz you're about to take is aimed at helping you determine the positive lifestyle choices you're already making. It may also help you identify the areas where your lifestyle is more adult-driven than child-friendly. Once you're able to recognize the areas of your life that are potentially making your child's behavior more chal-lenging, you'll be able to create a plan for change. Perhaps you already make sleep a major priority in family life; if so, wonderful. Since this area of your lifestyle requires little change, you might instead choose to work on providing healthier nutrition or examine family relationships. Whatever the quiz reveals, take this opportu-nity to see where you are and plan where you're going. Take the time to take the last of the three quizzes, "Is your lifestyle adult-driven or child-friendly?"

Is your lifestyle adult-driven or child-friendly?

— — —

This quiz is intended to raise your awareness about the areas of your family's lifestyle that need improvement. While your lifestyle decisions are yours alone, your child will learn best and behave better if expectations around lifestyle are child-friendly. Exceptions can be made to routines, and at times there may be family dynamic issues you can't do much about, but adding structure to your child's life will help him to be successful in his relationships at home, at school, and in the neighborhood.

DIRECTIONS

Give yourself one point for each statement that is true for your child.

Activity and Routines

My child . . .

___Enjoys some physical activity every day

___Plays more often with imaginative or creative toys/activities than with screens (TV, video games, computers)

___Participates in fewer than three playgroups, classes, clubs, or organizations per week

___Is expected to change locations fewer than five times per day

___Has the same child-care arrangement or after-school supervision each day

___Eats meals at about the same time each day

___ Eats dinner each night before he is tired

Total Score _____

Sleep and Rest

My child . . .

___ Has a simple, consistent bedtime routine

___ Goes to sleep the same time each night

___ Goes to sleep in the same bed each night

___ Has no technology such as a TV or computer in his room

___ Rarely comes to me in the middle of the night

___ Wakes up in the morning on his own in a good mood

___ Has an opportunity each day to take a nap or spend some quiet time relaxing

Total Score _____

Nutrition

My child . . .

___ Eats breakfast each day

___ Eats fruits and vegetables

___ Eats more protein and high-fiber foods than carbohydrates and high-sugar foods

___ Eats fewer than three snack foods per day

___ Drinks more milk and water than soda and juice

____Eats more home-cooked meals than prepared, restaurant, and take-out foods combined

____Joins the family meal at least three times per week

Total Score _____

Family Relationships

My child . . .

____Has the same set of expectations for behavior from both parents

____Rarely sees her parents argue

____Spends more time with her parents than with child-care providers

____Has parents who travel for work fewer than twice per month

____Is exposed to overnight houseguests fewer than twice per month

____Has generally peaceful relationships with his siblings

____Enjoys at least one fun family activity each week

Total Score _____

SCORE EACH CATEGORY

Activity and Routines Score   _____

Sleep and Rest Score   _____

Nutrition Score   _____

Family Relationships Score   _____

If you scored 6–7 points in a given category

A commitment to a child-friendly family situation is obvious. This aspect of your family's lifestyle is clearly important to you. Great job! You're making positive lifestyle choices in this category. Your child-friendly ways will positively impact behavior and learning.

If you scored 2–5 points in a given category

Family life is complicated. You and your child will be expected to be spontaneous and handle many ups and downs related to everyday living. If you are concerned about your child's behavior, your lifestyle choices in this category may be playing a role. Take credit for the positive lifestyle choices you are already making and try to make changes in the areas where your lifestyle and your child's capabilities are out of sync.

If you scored 0–1 points in a given category

Life is tough. Many parents fear their child has special needs, a challenging temperament, or developmental issues when an adult lifestyle imposed on a child may be the real problem. I strongly urge you to begin modifying your lifestyle in child-friendly ways. You can develop a proactive plan for making any area of lifestyle more of a priority. Even small changes make a big difference.

This quiz was developed in collaboration with Tom Griffin.

Spoil the Child

You've taken all three quizzes. You know your predominant parenting style. You have a better sense of, or maybe better language to describe your child's style of behavior. Now you know which aspects of your lifestyle are adult-driven and those that are child-friendly. If you found numerous aspects of your lifestyle geared more toward you than your child, this could be significantly impacting your child's behavior.

Rebecca took the lifestyle quiz and thought it really opened her eyes to some of her child's behavior. "Danvers is a very sweet little boy. But I'd been worried lately about how emotional he can get. Sometimes he gets so easily frustrated he throws things or he'll burst out crying over something silly."

When Rebecca took the lifestyle quiz, she found she's already making child-friendly choices in the activities and routines and family relationships sections of the quiz. But she found the sleep and rest and nutrition portions of the quiz pointed out areas with room for improvement. "I can see now where even some simple changes to his bedtime routine and the types of foods he eats will help him behave better and become less frustrated during the day."

The lifestyle quiz is intended to do a number of things for you as you parent. Generally, I want to raise awareness about what every child needs in family life to behave his or her best. Specifically, you can use the quiz to guide the changes you'd like to make to your own lifestyle. And finally, it can serve as a means for you to take a stand against the pressure others will direct your way, encouraging you to live in ways that are counterproductive to your child's well-being.

Achieving a balance between your needs and desires and creating a child-friendly lifestyle should be your goal. No matter how many changes you make moving from an adult-driven lifestyle to a child-friendly one, family life will never be child-friendly every minute of every day. Things never run smoothly all the time, and no parent is perfectly able to anticipate all the ins and outs and ups and downs of running a household and raising a child. Life happens. Holidays come and work deadlines are imposed. Vacations change daily routines. Your mother-in-law will come to visit. Strive for balance.

The next time you want to go out to dinner on a Saturday night and you're thinking about taking your child, ask yourself: "Is this going to work for my child?" If you can predict you're heading for a dinner disaster, you can prevent the calamity by making one of many child-friendly choices: get

> *Whether you predict and prevent or predict and practice, take charge making it clear who is the adult and who is the child.*

take out, get a babysitter, or go out to breakfast instead. Or you can prepare your child for your expectations and practice the acceptable behavior you're looking for. Anyone want to play restaurant?

Whichever choice you make, your child is allowed to be a child. If you choose not to take your child, your child isn't forced to endure a situation he doesn't have the skills to manage; he isn't expected to behave well in an environment meant for adults. And if you do choose to take your child, you'll have provided the tell-me, show-me discipline that increases the likelihood he'll succeed in that environment; he will have had the chance to practice and skill-build. Whether you predict and prevent, or predict and practice, take charge making it clear who is the adult and who is the child. Spoil your son or daughter with a child-friendly lifestyle. It's something your child really wants you to do and something from which you will reap countless benefits, too.

12. Creating a Child-Friendly Lifestyle

Bobby works hard to maintain his new home located on a main street in a revitalized part of the city. A self-proclaimed do-it-your-selfer, he's planted all new shrubs in the front yard and he's fenced in the backyard so his boys will be safe when they play outside. One morning, one of Bobby's boys finds a baseball in the backyard. Since Bobby's property is next to a vacant lot, he assumes the ball was tossed into the yard by some neighborhood boys who were playing there last night. Bobby sees no harm in letting his son have the baseball, so he lets him keep it. Off his son goes to play ball with his brother in their own backyard.

Days later, Bobby's boys find another baseball and two tennis balls. Bobby still sees no harm in his boys playing with what's been tossed into the yard. One morning, as Bobby's heading out to work he notices several beer cans have been tossed over the fence and into his side yard. He collects the cans and tosses them into the trash can between his property and the vacant lot. Bobby wasn't bothered by the baseballs and tennis balls tossed into his backyard but the beer cans are another matter. He doesn't want his boys to see the cans, play with them, or even ask questions about the cans. So now each morning before Bobby goes to work, he surveys his property looking for what he'll allow into his yard and what he'll need to toss back.

For Bobby it was baseballs and beer cans. For you it might be toys you like or toys you don't like, language you'll allow or language that offends. There are movies the whole family can enjoy and those with themes inappropriate for your young viewers. No matter how old your child is, things are being thrown into your backyard, too. And you'll need to decide what should stay and what must go.

Back to Basics

Everybody else is _____ . You can fill in the blank: eating more, sleeping less, wearing this, or doing that. Your lifestyle is highly influenced by other families' lifestyle choices along with the media's image of typical family life today. Unfortunately, much of what's being forced on you may not be that good for you but it's really not good for your child. More stress for you equals more stress for your child.

It's Christmas and nine-month-old baby Sal will be meeting many family members for the first time. Enzo and Lenora's first Christmas with Sal will begin with a car trip, traveling more than 250 miles from their home to begin the visit with Lenora's family. Once they arrive at their first stop, staying from December twenty-third until Christmas morning, Enzo, Lenora, and Sal will go from casual get-togethers to elaborate holiday celebrations. They'll sleep at Lenora's sister's home, where she lives with her husband and five sons. In the afternoon of Christmas Day, they'll get back in the car and travel one hundred miles farther from where they live to Enzo's family home for Christmas dinner and gift giving. They'll sleep over night at Enzo's grandparents' home and finally, they'll begin their return trip home.

Though Enzo and Lenora wanted very much to introduce their beautiful baby to family, they had reservations about the trip before it began. Reassured by her mother on every doubt, Lenora was convinced everything would be fine. But during the trip, nine-month-old Sal was apprehensive with each new person he met, crying and sticking to Lenora like glue. Though Sal hadn't minded being in the car during short trips near home, the roughly seven-hundred-mile round-trip car ride, though broken up over several days, got worse by the mile. The trip included many different locations. It seemed just when they were settled it was time to move locations again. The visit introduced Sal to many new people, making his developmentally expected separation anxiety more pronounced. The festivities were loud, long, and overstimulating for Sal. Some family members dismissed Sal's difficulty, chocking it up to a busy visit. Others considered Sal a fussy baby, one who couldn't go with the flow. Enzo and Lenora were disappointed family members didn't see their normally easygoing baby, a boy with big grins and easy laughter.

Have you ever been expected to participate in a family gathering, one you know will be hard for you to handle, never mind your child? Long-distance travel, high social expectations, unusual foods, and different beds. Altering your child's routines may meet the needs of your family or friends, but what does it do for you as a parent? And what does it do to your child?

Enzo and Lenora agreed their trip was a disaster. By the time they returned home, Sal was so overtired he fell asleep the minute his little body was placed in his crib. For days following the trip, Sal was out of sorts. Reestablishing pre-trip routines such as napping during the day, eating at regular intervals, and sleeping well at night took a lot out of Sal and his parents. Enzo and Lenora wondered, was it worth it?

Have you ever found yourself in Enzo and Lenora's situation, forced to make a tough decision?

Simple means respecting the basics: solid structure, predictable routines, good nutrition, regular fitness, lots of sleep, time to relax and a few healthy relationships.

Do you make other people's needs the priority, succumbing to the pressure to change your family's lifestyle in ways you know will bring more conflict or challenging behavior your way? Sometimes you'll say yes. When you do, by all means step back and anticipate what tampering with routines like mealtime, bedtime, and social time will do to your child. If you do choose to raise your behavioral expectations, prepare as best you can and be compassionate to your child. If you go into situations unprepared and your child has difficulty rising to the challenge, you may be tempted to get angry with him for behaving poorly even though he behaved as you expected he would.

You can, of course, just say no. While you might choose to toss your child-friendly lifestyle to the wind for a yearly holiday or the occasional vacation, it's not something you want to do as a general rule. Though it's not easy to resist the pressure others impose on you to engage in an adult-driven lifestyle, it *will* adversely affect your child. Remember, simple is better. Simple means respecting the basics: solid structure, predictable routines, good nutrition, regular fitness, lots of sleep, time to relax, and a few healthy relationships. With a simple child-friendly lifestyle, even at the holidays or on vacation, your child will feel good and behave well. And when he does, everyone is happier, including you.

If She Can Predict It, She Can Behave

Dessert comes after dinner. Teeth are brushed before bed. Socks first, then shoes. Many aspects of daily life are routine and therefore predictable. Simply because your child carries out these habits repeatedly, he recognizes these practices as rules or fences. On occasion, you might serve dessert before dinner or put your child to bed without brushing his teeth—not on the same night, of course—but these are exceptions to your rules, fences with open gates.

Expressions like *the exception to the rule* or *rules are meant to be broken* exist because there are times in life when exceptions are called for. But your child will behave best if there are more predictable fences and fewer exceptions. Your child will be more capable of accepting your fences when life is repetitive enough and routine enough to be predictable. In short, your child should find the fence gate closed more often than he finds the gate open.

Lois likes to run a tight ship; being organized comforts her and helps her manage the stress of day-to-day living. She serves breakfast and dinner to five-year-old Mae and seven-year-old Ginny at roughly the same time each day. Bedtime rarely changes. The children take the bus to school each morning and go to ballet class every Thursday. Mae is an energetic, outgoing child and like her mother, prefers predictable routines. Ginny is described by her mother as a child more capable of going-with-the-flow.

Your child will be more capable of accepting your fences when life is repetitive enough and routine enough to be predictable.

The week prior to school letting out for summer was filled with field days, book fairs, and ice cream socials. Lois and the girls were looking forward to spending a carefree summer together. Two days after the last day of school, Lois and her family take an early summer vacation and return just in time to celebrate Mae's birthday.

By July, Lois is concerned about Mae's behavior. Almost every day she gets agitated over some small disappointment or friendship misunderstanding. She storms to her room crying about the unfairness of life. In the late afternoon, she's queasy and at night she has difficulty falling asleep.

The last week of school. The first days of summer. Vacations. Birthdays. Are these out-of-the-ordinary days cause for celebration or are they the days of the year when the routines on which your child has come to lean all but disappear? Mae, who's come to rely on her mother's everyday schedule and ordinary comings and goings, is reacting to her mother's new fences. These summer fences are unpredictable, perhaps more spontaneous and irregular than either her age or temperament can manage.

Does every day need to look and feel the same to your child? Certainly not. But you'll want generally predictable mealtimes, bedtimes, playtimes, homework sessions, and social gatherings. And should your plans need to change, prepare your child in advance for what will be different and what will stay the same. If you're going to make an exception to the rule, be sure to let your child know ahead of time. Your child will benefit because she'll be prepared for the changes in expectation. You'll benefit because your child will know you're opening the gate just this once; you're not creating a new fence forever.

Elsie brings nine-year-old Rosie to a math tutor every Tuesday afternoon. Six-year-old Hunter tags along for the ride because he must. Usually, Elsie uses the time she's waiting for Rosie to read to Hunter or do brief errands. One Tuesday, when Elsie knows Hunter hasn't eaten much lunch and is complaining he's thirsty, she decides to stop at a local eatery to get Hunter a milk shake. Before she gets up to the order window, she bends down and builds a fence. "Hunter, I'm happy to get you a vanilla shake today but we won't be doing this every Tuesday. Repeat after me, getting a milk shake today is an exception."

Changes to your daily, weekly, monthly routines can be spontaneous and fun. And they don't need to create havoc. But keep in mind, unless you're willing to permanently change your fences or the freedoms you offer in the backyard, be sure to help your child recognize you're fully aware you've opened the gate. And don't forget to let him know exactly when it's about to close once more. Exceptions can certainly be made. But the child who's able to settle into child-friendly routines, ones that change infrequently and only with good reason, feels safe and secure. By providing your child with this safety and security you've met one of your child's most basic needs: the need for love and care.

You Are What You Eat

Another of your child's basic needs is for good, healthy nutrition—emphasis on the words *good* and *healthy*. Ask any nutritionist or physician and they'll tell you today's generation, capable of negotiating burgers and fries from their parents, will indeed get much more than they've asked for. With high obesity rates and diseases such as adult onset diabetes now being diagnosed in young children, some experts project this will be the first generation to live a shorter lifespan than the previous generation.

Does your child's typical food intake include white pasta, white rice, bagels, or snack foods like chips and pretzels and cookies? Does your child eat mostly processed foods like chicken nuggets, frozen pizza, or fish sticks? All of these foods break down in your child's body into increased amounts of sugar. When you put lots of sugar into your child's body, his blood sugar goes up and then in a short time goes back down, making him believe he's hungry again.

Eating foods of poor quality actually makes your child overeat. Eating snack foods high in sugar and fat trains your child to dislike high-quality foods. Foods rich in flavor become perceived as too bitter or too spicy. Foods of high quality build strong bone and muscle, maintain healthy weight and make your child feel happy and satisfied. And for the child struggling to behave well, good nutrition is even more critical.

Evelyn has engaged in table tactics with her eight-year-old son Justin since he was a baby. He won't eat this, he doesn't like that. His food repertoire includes muffins, macaroni and cheese, grapes, lemonade, hot dogs, and grilled cheese. And of course cookies, crackers, doughnuts, and candy. There have been times when Evelyn is so concerned her son hasn't consumed enough calories, Justin's been able to negotiate ice cream for dinner.

Justin's poor nutrition is something that concerns Evelyn, but she doesn't see how she can change it. She's been told by friends he'll become more adventurous with his food choices when he's older. She's certainly had her share of food fights with Justin to "just try a bite." In the long term, her son's nutrition is affecting his health. In the short term, it's affecting his behavior.

Justin's described by many as a boy with a short fuse, hot-tempered, and prone to crying about the ordinary mishaps of childhood. After talking with Evelyn, she was able to describe patterns of difficult, edgy behavior occurring most often in late morning, late afternoon, and at bedtime.

Though Justin is hardwired to be more intense and sensitive, his poor nutrition is contributing to his difficult behavior. When you work toward temperament, it means factoring in all the things you can do to make behavior better. Healthy nutrition makes everyone behave better.

The proactive plan for changing Justin's nutrition started with Evelyn knowing when to talk and when not to. If good nutrition isn't negotiable, Evelyn needs to build strong fences early and then keep them up at mealtime. She started by teaching Justin about healthy foods, but she didn't do it during mealtime.

Fuel food is the food he needs to eat the most; this is the food that makes his body function effectively. Fuel food includes healthy protein such as chicken, fish, nuts, beans, cheese, and milk. It includes grains high in fiber such as whole-wheat breads and whole-grain cereals. More vegetables, less fruit. More water, less juice. Then there are the fun foods. Everyone enjoys snacks and treats but these foods should be limited to once or twice a day and never eaten when you're hungry.

Evelyn and Justin go grocery shopping. Together they made a list of foods Justin knows he likes and foods he's willing to try. Evelyn agrees to always serve a salad—which he likes—with dinner, as well as have five staple foods always on hand in case the meal she offers isn't one Justin cares for. Evelyn lets her son know she will no longer negotiate food choices with him. When dinner rolls around, if he objects to what she's serving, after he eats his salad, he may get up and choose one of the five agreed-upon foods. Their list included yogurt, carrots, peanut butter on whole-wheat bread, milk, and cheese; they put this list on the refrigerator.

In less than one week, Justin added to his list many more foods he enjoyed, ones Evelyn had been serving to the rest of the family. Once the negotiation over food stopped, Justin accepted the concept of fuel food and fun food and is now a much better eater.

Time for dinner, time to stop talking. Are you doing all your teaching about healthy eating *while* you're eating? The proactive work done to teach healthy nutrition and prepare your child for mealtime is critical and will decrease conflict. But your child's experience—if it's anything like Justin's—may be encouraging him to negotiate at mealtime. If fighting over food is not negotiable, the talking is over. During dinner, just point to your list of acceptable foods on the refrigerator. If your child wants to eat, he will eat.

Are you worried he won't? No need to. As long as your child is on the growth chart for his height and weight, a missed meal is a small price to pay to change poor nutrition into healthy eating habits. If your child is not on the growth chart for height and weight or has a chronic illness, creating a fence for good nutrition should be done with guidance from your child's doctor.

Whose Bedtime Is It, Anyway?

While every child will benefit from predictable routines and healthy nutrition, there is no more powerful predictor of behavior than a child's sleep pattern. Your child's daytime behavior is directly and strongly linked to the sleep she gets. And not just the previous night's sleep either; sleep lost on Sunday night can affect her behavior through Tuesday. You can't make your child sleep but you can set your child up to make getting a night of good sleep more likely. By building fences aimed at going to bed at the right time under the right circumstances, you'll decrease bedtime battles and middle-of-the-night interruptions, helping your child sleep better and behave well.

Ernie's wife works the second shift, so putting four-year-old Bertha to bed each night is his sole responsibility. Bertha acts tired at dinnertime, which is anytime between 6:00 and 7:30 P.M., but by bedtime she's as wound up as a top. Her second wind makes every task more time-consuming and more emotionally charged. Brushing teeth, picking books, and staying in bed take so long, Ernie is ready for bed by the time she has settled for the night. The negotiations taking place at bedtime have a telling effect on Bertha during the day, too. But the why behind her behavior is seen as something else entirely.

Preschool teachers say Bertha can't focus on her arts and crafts projects; she's easily distracted. During free playtime, she gets so wired it's next to impossible to calm her down. It's getting so that one teacher needs to be near her at all times because she's been known to push and shove other children to get her own way.

Bertha is among thousands of little ones whose behavior is so challenging, parents and teachers question the presence of a behavioral diagnosis when lack of sleep is the real culprit. When you're tired, you drag. When your child is tired, she gets any combination of agitated, hyperactive, restless, or energetic. But she can't necessarily say she's tired; only the older child can recognize what tired feels like and still may not admit she's tired.

The proactive plan for creating a healthier sleep pattern begins with knowing when to talk and when to act. During the day, Ernie tells Bertha what the new bedtime routine will look like. First, he'll back dinner up to 5 P.M., which will probably solve some mealtime issues, but is really aimed at getting Bertha through the bedtime routine before she gets that second wind. The routine will include brushing teeth and putting on jammies right after dinner. The earlier she does these necessary tasks, the better, since she'll be more cooperative if she's not already overtired. Next she'll choose her two stories between a handful of books rather than from the entire bookcase. Once she's tucked in bed, she's expected to stay there.

Ernie knows the new fence for bedtime will get pushed the first night. After all, it's been Bertha's experience that fences for bedtime are negotiable. When she pushes for more stories, she gets more stories. When she resists going to bed, she gets more of Ernie's time. So why wouldn't she try to kick the gate open?

Since Ernie can predict it, he can prevent it. And he does. Long before bedtime, he tells Bertha if she gets out of bed he won't talk, he'll just walk her back. When it's bedtime, it's bedtime. Ernie knows now—if it's not negotiable—the talking is over.

In a matter of a few nights Bertha accepted the new bedtime fence. And after two weeks, her teachers at preschool said Bertha was a different child. She was cooperative and played well with others. Her ability to focus and accept frustration when working on projects was remarkable. Sleep is a wonderful thing.

Simple routines and consistent nonverbal responses to bedtime fence pushing are crucial for the young child. Whether it's when your child goes to bed or middle-of-the-night awakenings, your follow-through should look the same. Prepare your child during the day by talking and role-playing, but once the fence is pushed, your actions will speak louder than anything you can verbalize.

If your child is older, healthy sleep patterns are just as important. Your child's school performance and behavior with friends is influenced by the amount and quality of his sleep. Regardless of your child's age, he should go to sleep the same time each night, and probably much earlier than you think. Your adolescent needs eight to nine hours of sleep to perform at his best. Resist the pressure to have any technology such as a TV or computer in his room. Technology in bedrooms is a problem for many reasons, including the effect on sleep. Television watching and computer use right before bed actually interferes with falling asleep, and contributes to vivid dreaming. Watch the exceptions you make to staying up late, drinking caffeine, or consuming sugar before bed. When your child is overstimulated right before bed or sleep schedules are altered even slightly, you make it harder for your child to get to sleep and stay asleep.

Healthy sleep habits taught to your child mean more sleep or more free time in the evening for you. I don't know any parent who would refuse either of those things. It's just a proactive plan away.

Play Is Work and Work Is Play

Your child may play soccer on a team or flute in the band. But does your child *play?* Building a fort in the living room. Creating an obstacle course in the driveway. Organizing a game of cards in the kitchen. The unstructured and unscheduled time of childhood provides valuable opportunities for learning.

On a sunny summer day, Gina doesn't have camp, she doesn't have art class, and she doesn't have swimming lessons. Gina is bored. If Gina could, she would plop down on the couch for a marathon of sitcoms or cozy up to the computer screen to write e-mail or browse websites. Instead, Gina's mother, Hazel, helps her daughter tap into the lost art of figuring out what she can do when presented with unstructured time.

Hazel brings Gina down to the side of the basement that houses all her old toys and art supplies. Hazel proposes Gina look for a neglected puzzle or paint set, something she can use to occupy the afternoon. An hour after her suggestion, Hazel finds Gina playing with some dolls she once cherished. "Don't tell anyone, okay Mom? My friends would make fun of me." Hazel tells Gina she played with her dolls until she was much older than Gina and her own mother shielded her from teasing, too.

What Gina learned that day was more important than what any television show or e-mail could've taught her. She learned to be creative and fill her free time with a productive activity, one that challenged her to lose herself in her imagination. It doesn't matter how old you are, creative imaginative play is just as important as any skill gained from a structured activity or class.

There are two types of activities that are cause for concern, especially if your child engages in them too often. The first type is structured activity. As discussed earlier, your young child doesn't need numerous classes, lessons, and clubs. Free play structured by you, right in your own backyard, will do as much to enhance development and learning as any class. It's your older child, especially during adolescence, who should be engaged in structured, adult-supervised activities.

> *Once you bring technology into your backyard, be prepared: You will need powerful fences to contain it.*

The second type of activity creating havoc with your child's development is technology. Video games, computer games, and techno toys interfere with the development of parts of your child's brain, while doing little to enhance creativity, teach effective social interaction, or lengthen attention span for anything techno-free, such as lessons in school or the process of homework. Technology exists and your child will be exposed to it, but you need to create fences with the knowledge that it does get in the way of certain aspects of social, emotional, physical, and cognitive development.

How much technology is too much technology? A child under three doesn't need any technology such as computer or video games to play well and have fun. Small amounts of carefully chosen television can be part of your young child's day, though none is even better.

The fences you build for television and technology-oriented toys are up to you. Technology teaches cause and effect; if I press this button, I get this result. Put off the use of instant messaging, e-mail, handheld computer games, and video games as long as you possibly can because any kind of technology can be addictive. Once you bring technology into your backyard, be prepared: You will need powerful fences to contain it.

There's No Place like Home

Your child asked you and you said no; he asked Dad, who said yes. Have you ever been part of this triangle? It might be easier to get one parent's fence gate open than the other's, so your child *will* gravitate toward the less reactive, more wavering parent to get what he needs or wants. No doubt the dynamics within your family—for better or worse—influence behavior. Whether you're living together or living apart, the expectations you have of your child, if different, will affect the way your child accepts fences.

Jesse and Brooke struggle to communicate over many things, one of which is parenting six-year-old Aiden. The latest disagreement centers on how to play in the neighborhood. Jesse thinks Aiden should toughen up when it comes to dealing with a particular boy who bosses him around. Brooke makes excuses for Aiden, thinking her baby needs more protection from this neighborhood bad boy. Aiden receives mixed messages every day, depending on who's supervising the play. Dad says if he hits you, hit him back. Mom says use your words. Aiden is mystified about how to manage. Today, Mom and Dad start arguing over Aiden's best options. Neither one notices that Aiden has gone to his room in tears.

When you and your child's other parent have the same set of expectations for behavior, life is good. When you don't, your child is either confused or uses this to his advantage. Being able to recognize the similarity in your fences and then getting each fence reinforced by more than one person teaches your child more consistently and quickly the expectations for behavior in your family.

You can't expect to agree with your child's other parent all the time about every parenting decision. But you certainly want to come to agreement the majority of time and do so without putting your child in the middle. At each developmental stage, there will be new issues to feel your way around. Is your child ready to move from a crib to a bed? Would your child be safe walking to school? Is she old enough to date? These and many more questions should be answered by both parents in the best interest of your child. The child you must nurture together, the child whose character will be shaped by both of you.

The reality is that parenting in sync is hard when you're together and even harder when you're apart. Whether you figure out how to do so on your own or with professional guidance, do whatever you can to agree on nonnegotiable fences and then follow through consistently. Your child is worth doing whatever it takes.

Parenting together is one of the most taxing of family issues. But if your child's behavior is inappropriate, out-of-control, or generally disruptive, you'll also need to examine how much time is spent in child care with inconsistent care providers and the effect your work schedule has on your child's sleep and nutrition. If your work life relates to your home life in ways that are more adult-driven than child-friendly, changes in your child's lifestyle could make a big difference.

Parents work. Sometimes overtime or travel is required. Parents get sick; sometimes the illness is minor, other times quite serious. Parents don't always get along and sometimes they divorce. Family life isn't always smooth sailing. There are times when transitions, disruptions, and inconsistencies can't be helped. But do your best to try to limit transitions, minimize upheavals, and stay consistent.

> *Home isn't just a place your child lives. It's the place where security—love—is found. It's the place where learning about relationships begins. It's the place you want your child to come back to, today and tomorrow.*

At every age, your child is influenced by family life, both the best and worst of it. The more positive family lifestyle choices you make, the better. Home isn't just a place your child lives. It's the place where security—love—is found. It's the place where learning about relationships begins. It's the place you want your child to come back to, today and tomorrow.

What's in Your Backyard?

Making your own lifestyle choices is hard enough. Where should you live? What should you do for work? Who will share your life? Then you have a child.

Now you must make lifestyle choices for someone new. Someone who hasn't learned yet what choices will suit her. The lifestyle choices she'll need to feel good and make good decisions are unclear to her at first. She needs you to show her the way.

The word *supervision* has two meanings. The first general meaning relates to care and protection. When your child is an infant or toddler, your supervision is direct. You follow her around making certain she doesn't put anything in an electrical outlet or go near the stairs. For most parents, once a child is more verbal, direct supervision drops off dramatically. It's as if once she can talk, it's assumed she's got the ability to make good decisions. And nothing is further from the truth.

Verbal skills, or the ability to communicate, are only one small piece of the decision-making puzzle. Your child needs your care and protection always, at every age. The size of your young child's backyard starts off small. Then you increase the freedoms found there as your child matures, demonstrating her ability to accept your fences. But beware of giving your child more freedom than she can handle.

Fifteen-year-old Trinity has a seventeen-year-old boyfriend, Michael. Trinity's mother, Etta, and her daughter talk often about the ups and downs of dating. Etta is very proactive about the fences she creates for Trinity. And Trinity accepts them.

Each weekend, Trinity and Michael go to friends' homes to watch movies and talk. Trinity tells her mother there's never any alcohol there and parents are always home. Though Trinity has earned her mother's trust because she accepts limits and acts in responsible ways, Etta has a practice of calling ahead to talk directly to a parent to be sure Trinity is in healthy social situations.

It's Saturday night and Trinity and Michael will be going to a friend's house they've been to many times before. After several weeks of calling and confirming parental supervision there, Etta decides this time she doesn't need to make the call. Later that night, Etta realizes she's made a mistake.

Thirty minutes after her ten o'clock curfew, Trinity and Michael erratically pull into the driveway. When Michael drops Trinity off at night he typically doesn't come inside; Etta is concerned so she heads out to the driveway. It's clear Trinity and Michael have been drinking. Etta gets both inside. She doesn't lecture. She doesn't react. She does assure them they'll discuss the situation later when they're better able to think and understand the ramifications of their choice to drink. She calls Michael's parents.

Supervision for your older child is tricky. You can't follow her around like you could when she was a toddler. Inevitably, your ability to protect becomes more indirect. But it should never be so indirect it's absent.

The second general meaning of the word *supervision* is to provide direction, to show the path or right course. Etta was proactive on many levels before Trinity and Michael went out each Saturday. And she was proactive still, when she found they'd made a mistake, putting themselves in an unacceptable situation. She didn't waver in her belief; underage drinking is unacceptable. She didn't react by yelling or even discussing the situation with teenagers who'd been drinking. Etta chose the RITE response. First, get them safe. Later when they're sober, discuss the situation and share with them the changes that will be made to future fences. Show the path. Direct the course.

The next day, Etta and Michael's parents sat down with Trinity and Michael. They shared their disappointment with the decision to drink, especially to drink and drive. They let them talk about how the situation at the friend's house got out of control and together they reviewed other options they had for doing what was right and safe. Etta told them that for a time, Saturday social gatherings would be at her house. A place where supervision would be more direct. Where trust could be earned. Where they would be safe.

Never be afraid to readjust the size of the backyard based on your child's ability to handle the freedoms you offer. Don't negotiate away your power to parent. Know when to talk and when to act. Don't let others sway you from doing what's right for your child.

With any kind of supervision, your child can be in the wrong place at the wrong time, something every parent fears. But you can do so much to monitor your child's backyard. You can watch what others are throwing into it and make decisions to keep the good and toss the rest. You can share openly and proactively with your child the reasons for your fences as well as all the freedoms to be found there. But never be afraid to readjust the size of the backyard based on your child's ability to handle the freedoms you offer. Don't negotiate away your power to parent. Know when to talk and when to act. Don't let others sway you from doing what's right for your child. You know your child best.

13. The Commitment to Stay Proactive

Marian has always loved being outside. As a young girl, she spent hours playing in her sandbox in summer. In autumn, like many children, Marian loved to rake leaves into a huge pile and then run and jump into the heap. She'd repeat the game over and over again, never tiring. In springtime, it was Marian who'd gravitate toward the puddles of rainwater that collected in her street, even if it meant she'd be covered in mud and have to contend with the disapproval of her parents.

It's no surprise to those who really know Marian that as an adult she continues to be drawn to the earth. Marian loves the time she spends in her garden. Several times a year, Marian reflects on the purpose of her plot. Does she continue to grow vines that climb over rockfaces, up and along the back fence? Which vegetables grow best in the raised beds and which don't thrive in the type of soil she's working with?

Each season, she reviews her budget for new plants, shrubs, and trees. Marian considers how much time she'll need to cultivate the soil, weed the garden, split overgrown plants, and replant them in other parts of her backyard. Sometimes Marian is forced to cut back a plant knowing her containment of it will benefit its growth in the long run.

The child of a proactive parent—a parent who has stepped out of the Negotiation Generation and one who knows when to talk and when to act—grows up to be a person of character.

Tending a garden requires time. The work, though predictable, is at times tedious, but reaps plentiful rewards. Marian lovingly and willingly chooses to tend to the plants in her backyard garden. And she isn't afraid to get her hands dirty.

Creating the best backyard for your child, one in which he can thrive, takes time, it's true. The way you ground your child with values and the way you nurture your child's skill development is complicated and time-consuming. You'll need to plan where fences get built, being careful to include age-appropriate freedoms within your backyard so your child isn't tempted to jump the fence.

With each developmental stage, you'll need to revisit the size and contents of your child's backyard to be sure it grows with his ever-changing capabilities. The work is hard indeed. The work you put into shaping your child's moral fiber, cultivating his capabilities, and training him to accept what is negotiable and what is not will yield great rewards, just like Marian's garden.

The child of a proactive parent—a parent who has stepped out of the Negotiation Generation and one who knows when to talk and when to act—grows up to be a person of character.

How Will You Play the Game?

No matter how you look at it, parenting takes time. But you *do* get to choose how you'll spend the time it takes to parent. Will you react to challenging behavior in the same way day after day, never really changing the dynamic between you and your child, spending time in predictable conflict? Or will you waver, never building the fences your child needs to feel safe, secure, and genuinely cared for, spending time worrying and waiting for what might happen next?

If you choose to spend your time parenting proactively, you'll reject the bad parent/bad child thinking of the blame game. Instead you'll recognize you can spend your time modifying your style, working toward your child's style, or refining your lifestyle, all with the goal of increasing family harmony.

A Chinese philosopher once said, "The journey of a thousand miles begins with a single step." What's the first step you're willing to take toward more family harmony? Perhaps you're willing to drop the rope of the power struggles that occur between you and your child. Maybe you'll begin by celebrating your child's strengths and work today to place one new skill in her bag. Or you might be ready to adopt a more child-friendly approach to your family's routine at dinner or bedtime. Though you may have a number of styles that could benefit from fine-tuning, wherever you choose to begin, start small.

Joaquin is the father of two daughters. With the birth of his first child, life for Joaquin didn't change much. While his wife stayed home to care for their baby daughter, he worked. He liked seeing himself as a family man, though he would've agreed he wasn't as involved in fathering as he'd expected.

> *No matter how you look at it, parenting takes time. But you do get to choose how you'll spend the time it takes to parent.*

After the birth of his second daughter, Joaquin's life became more stressful, especially as the girls grew older. He felt the pressure to work harder to make a good living for his family. And he felt he should be doing more at home: helping the girls with homework, cooking meals, and doing more laundry. Stress for Joaquin meant a shorter temper with the girls, and he took on the role of reactive father. After another night losing his cool with one of the girls, this time over her getting into pajamas, Joaquin realized it was time for him make some changes to his parenting style.

"I can't believe I yelled at a little girl over the kind of pajamas she should wear to bed. I'm the grown up and she's just a little girl. From here on in, I'm going to make a conscious choice not to take my frustrations out on my children. If I can manage a group of people at work, treating them with respect, I can certainly do the same for my girls."

Joaquin chose to start his journey toward more family harmony by examining his style and the impact his reactivity has on family life.

Confident her style of parenting is already fairly proactive, Christine has chosen to take her first step by skill-building with her five-year-old daughter, Ann. Independent and always willing to try new things, Ann is a dynamic child. Ann can be persistent. She's been known to do a very good job negotiating that which is not negotiable, yet Christine admits she's allowed her daughter to do a lot of talking about rules, even when they should've been hard and fast.

Christine spends time with Ann preparing her for the new way she'll need to accept fences. "Ann, you're smart and very clever so I'm going to share with you how things are going to change between us. Lately, the tone of your voice has been sharp and demanding. I want you to speak to me more respectfully. Let's talk about the ways you can ask me for things or talk with me in ways that sound much nicer."

Even when Christine is trying to be proactive about disrespectful behavior, Ann persists. She's pushing the fence faster than Christine can build it. "I don't want to talk about this, it's stupid. I talk to you just fine."

Christine didn't pick up the rope of the power struggle. She used one of my favorite techniques—one minute on the clock. "Ann, we will be having this conversation. But we'll have it respectfully. I'll wait one minute on the clock. After that, if you're respectful, we will continue."

Christine changed the dynamic she has with Ann when she refused to continue a proactive conversation after it descended into conflict. If she continued talking to Ann, she would be negotiating a nonnegotiable fence; she just said she wouldn't talk if Ann was being disrespectful. By waiting one minute on the clock before proceeding, Christine delivers the clear message that she's in charge. Trust me, a minute is a long time for a child to wait, especially when I'm certain Ann would prefer the conversation was over.

After one minute on the clock, Christine continued. "Ann, if you use a disrespectful tone with me, first I'll clear my throat as a reminder; if your tone of voice continues to hurt my feelings, I'll leave the room. But I won't talk to you if you speak to me in disrespectful ways. Instead, my actions will tell you all you need to know. Now let's practice the respectful ways you can ask me for what you need."

The first step Christine took was to modify the skills Ann has in her bag; skills she'll need for knowing when to persist and when to let go.

Elisabeth is a true entrepreneur; she's single-handedly opened a clothing boutique in her town. While she's just becoming a successful business owner, she's already a successful mother raising two young children. Always described as the most polite and cooperative children in child care, Elisabeth's three-year-old daughter and four-year-old son have recently been having trouble getting along with the other children at day care. Her daughter lashes out with her fists and her son with his words. It doesn't take any great reflection on Elisabeth's part to recognize the reason for the changes in her children's behavior.

"I have been expecting way too much from these very little children. Because I've needed to get the store ready to open, they've had late nights, lousy take-out, and less attention from me. I've decided something's gotta give and it can't be my children. Today I hired someone to help me at the store part-time, so at night I can make the children a good meal and put them to bed on time."

Elisabeth's journey begins with child-friendly modifications to her lifestyle.

Where will your journey begin?

Take Back Your Authority

It's been clearly established—parenting takes time. But it also takes plenty of another valuable resource—your energy. In order to be the positive authority your child needs, you need determination, patience, stamina, resilience, and sometimes courage. Parenting takes energy.

> *In order to be the positive authority your child needs, you need determination, patience, stamina, resilience, and sometimes courage. Parenting takes energy.*

Imagine your body contains a special place where the energy you need to parent is stored. Picture a precious jar of energy filled and refilled each day by you. All day, every day, you'll decide how your energy will be used. You'll decide how and when to replenish the energy you store in your precious jar. Some days you'll exhaust all the energy you have to parent early in the day because you're wasting it negotiating issues that shouldn't be negotiable. Other days you'll put more energy in the jar than you expend because you schedule time to do something for yourself like read a good book or take a long walk.

There are some things in life over which you have complete control, such as the way you choose to respond to your child. There are some things in life over which you only have some control, like what's happening to your child at school. And of course, there are some things in life you have no control over at all. The first step toward protecting your precious jar of energy is to recognize where you have complete control, where you have little, and where you have none. When you can distinguish between the things you'll be able to change and the things you're powerless over, doling out energy deliberately and carefully will make parenting much easier to do.

Margaret is the mother of two-year-old triplets, Henrietta, Hope, and Hugh. Energy to parent is something she'd buy if she could. When her children were very young, Margaret realized the way she allocated her most valuable resource—her energy—was the single most critical factor to her parenting success. As the mother of active young children, one of whom has special medical needs, busy doesn't begin to define her life.

"I can't waste an ounce of energy when it comes to caring for my children. I've devised the craziest ways of feeding them, getting them to bed, even playing with them. Everything I do is designed to save steps, time, or money. I still accept every offer of help I get. I sleep when they sleep; I even nap when they nap."

Margaret holds sacred the energy she has in her precious jar because she knows without it parenting will be next to impossible. Either because she knows this intuitively or because she's been forced to learn this while parenting triplets, Margaret recognizes some parenting choices build energy while other choices waste it.

Energy wasters include yelling and shouting—in short, being reactive to your child's behavior. Reacting to behavior includes giving commands from a distance, using negative language, and spending little or no energy anticipating predictable behavior. "Stop that." "Come here." "Don't you dare." If you're far away from your child when you're building fences and do so with negative language, she sees your fences as negotiable and her need to do as you say optional.

Talking too much during conflict tops the list as the biggest energy waster. The premise of this entire book is there is a time to talk and a time to act. When you talk in conflict, when you pick up the rope of a power struggle, you're negotiating that which is not negotiable. You're wasting the most valuable resource you have for parenting—the energy in your precious jar. Energy you'll need for later in the day. Energy only you can replenish.

Just as energy can be wasted, energy can be guarded and held for when you need it most. Energy builders include using small actions to deliver messages and using nonverbal cueing to convey meaning. When your child responds quickly and appropriately to your actions or nonverbal messages, you not only save energy you might otherwise have wasted talking about nonnegotiables, but you actually put energy back into your precious jar. Isn't it an amazing feeling when your child does what you want him to do the first time you put up a fence?

Anticipating predictable behavior, choosing either to prevent a challenging situation, or to prepare your child to behave well, are energy builders. When you parent proactively, you build skill. When you build skill out of a stressful situation, your child can behave better in the real situation. When your child behaves well after having been prepared by you and given an opportunity to practice with you, energy goes back in your precious jar.

In order to parent effectively, you must use time wisely and you must use energy wisely, too. Whether it's every day or every week, use some of your time to consciously put energy back into your precious jar. Your energy stores can be replenished by getting a good night's sleep or by exercising. You can read a wonderful book, write in a beautiful journal, talk to a treasured friend. You can cook, sing, garden, or pray. But you need to fill the jar with those activities that fill you up physically, emotionally, and spiritually. Without positive energy, parenting is harder; it's much more tempting to react or waver. When your precious jar is more full than empty, it's easier to be proactive.

Punish No More

What's your reaction to getting a speeding ticket? How do you feel when a store clerk scolds you for having sixteen items in the fifteen-item checkout line? No one enjoys being penalized. No one likes being reprimanded. Your child doesn't want you to resort to punishment to show him the error of his ways, either. He wants to do the right thing in the first place; he simply doesn't know how, at least not yet. To truly change your child's style of behavior, you'll need to start by seeing his temperament in a positive light and then skill-build—not punish—to get new ways of behaving in the bag.

> *To truly change your child's style of behavior, you'll need to start by seeing his temperament in a positive light and then skill-build—not punish—to get new ways of behaving in the bag.*

According to Bridget, her greatest strength is her ability to focus and be organized. That she should be the mother of ten-year-old Jude, who is easily distracted and highly disorganized, is ironic.

"I used to find myself getting really angry with Jude. I'd say

'Why can't you just pay attention?' 'You're just being lazy; clean up your mess.' But now I realize we're just cut from different cloth. He's not doing these things on purpose. He really doesn't know how to focus and get organized."

Bridget is right. Her organization is hard-wired in, just as his disorganization is in him. Her level of focused attention is biological, as is his distractibility. Though it might be frustrating for Bridget to be on the opposite end of the continuum from Jude, she's in a perfect position to help him get new skills for school success in the bag.

"Once I started looking at Jude's strengths, I realized the things I love most about him are the very things that at times frustrate me. I admire how he's able to see a million ways of doing something, but it drives me crazy when he won't make a decision. I love how he gets lost in playing his trumpet but I get mad when he plays right before school, losing track of time and missing the bus. I know I have some things I can teach him about being organized, especially for school. I'm starting to realize he has a lot to teach me about being creative, spontaneous, and thinking outside the box."

When you really examine your child's bag, you'll see as much, if not more, positive qualities than negative traits. Elements of temperament are neither right or wrong, good or bad. They're simply working for your child or not. Jude's bag, like your child's, is full of wonderful qualities that make him the unique person he is, and you don't want to change that. Certainly, he'll need you to help him smooth out traits, characteristics, or mannerisms that could be working better for him. There isn't a child in the world who couldn't use some new skills for doing better in school, managing social situations, or getting along more effectively at home.

Isolating your child with time-outs or groundings won't change the bag. Taking away toys or television won't change the bag.

Yelling, demeaning, and pleading won't change the bag. Skill-building, not punishment, changes the bag.

When you become familiar with your child's strengths along with his personal struggles to behave in more acceptable ways, you'll be able to feel great empathy for what it's like to walk in his shoes. When you're truly able to feel compassion for him, you won't want to punish his behavior any more.

> *When you become familiar with your child's strengths along with his personal struggles to behave in more acceptable ways, you'll be able to feel great empathy for what it's like to walk in his shoes.*

Take It On

Your child faces examples of boundary pushing many times every day. Some of her friends push boundaries in small ways like taking an extra dessert or going home from the movies ten minutes later than expected. Some of her friends push boundaries in more dangerous ways like drinking while driving or having sex with a boyfriend. All around her she sees others negotiating nonnegotiable boundaries with parents, teachers, and coaches whose job it is to build fences and keep those fences up, especially when they're pushed. It's only a matter of time before your child succumbs to the domino effect; if everybody else is doing it, why shouldn't she? Unless.

Unless you're really there to put up fences, mend fences, and together with your child take charge of what's being thrown in your backyard. When you partner with your child to manage the influences of other families and society in general on her thoughts, attitudes, and skills, your child won't be tempted to do what everybody else is doing and neither will you.

Colette and Francis have been friends since sixth grade. Now, with daughters of their own in sixth grade and different parenting styles, their friendship is changing.

"Did you hear about the sixth-grade formal?" asks Francis. "I think it's so cute. Some of the girls are going with dates. Hey, do you want to chip in for a limo for the girls?"

A sixth-grade formal dance. Dates for eleven-year-olds. Limousines for a dance. Colette can't believe what's being thrown in her backyard. Though her friend didn't utter the dreaded words, *everybody else is*, parent pressure is still ever present in their conversation. What will others think of Colette if her daughter doesn't have a date, a formal dress, or a limo? What in the world would they think of Colette if her daughter is the only girl who doesn't go? Colette would be viewed as too strict and no fun; she'd be preventing her daughter from sharing this experience with her friends.

It's hard to be in the minority on any parenting decision. Unfortunately, if you're in the minority today, it's probably the best litmus test you can use to determine if you're building the best fences for your child. In Colette's story, she feels on a gut level that eleven-year-olds neither can nor should try to navigate the adult world of dates and dances. Think about the natural result of putting your child in such a mature situation. Will she push more fences, wanting to get close to a boy she's had her eye on? This will only serve to move her further along the intimacy continuum and possibly get her closer to sexual experiences than either of you is prepared to handle. Or will she be the wallflower, feeling out of place and left out because the skills she has to manage this sophisticated social experience aren't in the bag yet? Whichever response your child might have, do you really want to put your child in such an awkward place just because other people chose to put their sons and daughters there?

I wish it were as simple as the *just say no* mantra you'll hear from some. You already know it's much harder than that to resist your child's fence pushing at the same time you refuse to give in to your friends' parent pressure. I'm not telling you to do anything I don't work hard to do myself.

Stand firm with me on slowing down the urge to rush your child through and past childhood. Find like-minded friends and family and then stick together. Offer more age-appropriate alternatives to the current trends that place a child in adult-driven situations only to leave parents wondering why things went awry. Build your own fences—personal boundaries—doing what's right for your child and your family. When you and I, and all the others who want to turn the tide, put child-friendly lifestyles before our adult desires, we'll be the majority and others will follow us.

You Know the Ropes

Picture me holding a pencil. Now imagine me telling you I'm thinking about writing on the wall. You don't want to waver or react; this is something you don't want me to do, you're clear about that. Since I've not drawn on the wall yet, you've got the power to influence my decision.

You could use positive words and clear gestures to direct me to place the pencil on the table. You could hand me some paper. While getting yourself a pencil and some paper, you could role-model using these objects appropriately, encouraging me to draw. Without talking at all, you could take my pencil.

Now let's say someone walks into the room and starts encouraging me to draw on the wall. "Go ahead, do it. I would if I were you."

For some, the addition of an outside influence on my behavior complicates the situation, making it feel like the odds I'll write on the wall just went way up. But I see it as simply a different situation to manage, one in which now you have additional options for influencing my decision. You can still do all the things you would've done had the situation not involved someone else, but now you have the power to influence the other person on my behalf. You could ask the person to stop influencing me. You could give this person paper and a pencil, too. Keep in mind I still haven't drawn on the wall, so you still have enormous power to influence my decision, as well as the ability to influence the other person's behavior.

Suddenly, the impulse to write on the wall can no longer be contained and I do it. Is there anything you can do now, to stop me from continuing? I'm afraid not. You're left with only a few options to set the situation straight. You can stop me from writing further by taking the pencil. You can hand me a sponge to clean up the mess I've made. Since your power to influence me proactively has passed, now your power lies in teaching me how to resolve the situation. Once the situation is recovered, you'll need to foresee whether or not I'll do this in the future. If you predict I will, you'll need to prevent this by confiscating pencils or by preparing me for how to manage the temptation to do this again.

The handwriting is on the wall. If only all parenting problems were as easy to solve, or as black and white, as taking away a pencil. The reality is the combination of your style, your child's style, and your lifestyle collide to make situations as simple as a pencil and the temptation to draw that much more emotionally charged. I assure you, if a child other than your own acted in ways you found unacceptable, you'd find it much easier to intervene with a calm and controlled response—the RITE response. It's true, writing on the wall is unacceptable, but you wouldn't waste a lot of energy from your precious jar to solve the predictable and often preventable behavior of another person's child. You'd know when to talk and when to act.

So with your child, use your power to influence wisely. Make a commitment to talk to your child in positive active ways, in advance of conflict. Communicate, don't lecture. Know what's negotiable and what's not. Resist the urge to pick up the rope, or drop it soon after you realize you have. Never be afraid to step in with action when your child needs to find the fence. Don't give away your power to parent.

It's Like Riding a Bike

Have you ever moved the location of your telephone or the place you keep your car keys? At first, you're fully aware of the new resting spots; after all, you consciously chose to move those items there. Later that day or even the next day, you'll find yourself going to the old location to get the phone or keys. Without conscious thought, you automatically go back to old places until you make the new places part of your regular thinking and behaving.

While you've been reading this book, focused on more proactive techniques for parenting, you've been traveling to a new place. Perhaps you've moved away from punishment and toward building better fences. Or maybe as you amble through your day, you're quicker to recognize when someone has picked up the rope and you're much more successful in dropping your end. Best of all would be that you're better able to share your child's journey, seeing his bag full of great traits and qualities, helping him smooth out the rough patches as he works his way through childhood. You don't need to punish; you will teach.

When you finish this book and move on to read that beautiful novel waiting for you on your bedside table, the ideas presented here will move out of your conscious thinking. If you've been successful adopting a few strategies like using small actions, not talking in conflict, or using role-play to prepare your child for difficult situations, then you've made these new parenting strategies automatic, habitual, unconscious. It's possible without conscious thought, at least at first, you'll slip back into your old style.

One day you'll notice you're reacting more, predicting less. Or you'll see your child pushing fences more and realize you're preparing him less. It's to be expected. Until your new style is truly automatic, you'll go back to your old one on occasion; just like you went back to the old place you kept your keys before the new place became etched in your mind.

Whether you lose your footing as you parent or your child goes down a path different from the one you'd wish he'd taken, neither of you will ever have to start your journey back at the beginning.

On a cool summer morning, Theresa and James plan a bike riding trip. Seven-year-old James has just recently learned to ride his bike without training wheels. Though eager to go, he's apprehensive. His mother, Theresa, expects the trip to have its ups and downs but she's prepared to support James and make the trip memorable. After they pack a backpack with snacks and water and review the safety rules, they hop on their bikes and ride.

Fifteen minutes into the bike trip going downhill, James hits a bump in the road and falls off his bike. Checking to be certain he's not hurt, Theresa comforts James with a hug and a kiss. Then she reviews his options and readies him to get back on the bike to finish the trip. James falls off his bike once more. Again, Theresa helps him get back on his bike, right in the place where he lost his balance.

Whether you lose your footing as you parent or your child goes down a path different from the one you'd wish he'd taken, neither of you will ever have to start your journey back at the beginning. Every single change you've already made to your style, your child's style, and your lifestyle informs the parenting decisions you'll make next.

Learning to be a proactive parent is like learning to ride a bike.

It might be challenging at first because you're not yet comfortable with it. At times, it will be effortless, pleasurable, and fun. Other times it will be an uphill climb; you'll be tired and wonder if you can do what it takes to get to the other side. There will be times you'll fall, like James, or maybe you'll lose your way. But you'll never have to start back at the beginning to get back on track. You'll pick yourself up, chart a new course, and continue on down the road.

Index